We Bought YOU

An Adoption $tory
That $trikes at Your $oul

By
William Power

We Bought YOU: An Adoption Story That Strikes at Your Soul
© 2025 William Power

This is a work of creative nonfiction. Certain names, locations, and identifying details have been changed or fictionalised to protect the privacy of individuals. Any resemblance to real persons, living or deceased, is coincidental and not intended by the author.

First Edition
Published by Aussie Guy's Books
Cover and Interior Design: Aussie Guy's Books
Author Website: aussieguysbooks.com.au

ISBN: 978-1-7642115-4-3
Printed Internationally with POD Services

Publisher's Note
The opinions expressed in this work are those of the author.
This book is intended as a personal narrative and reflection on the lived experience of adoption, trauma, and recovery.

Readers seeking support for issues raised in this book are encouraged to contact a qualified mental health professional or local support services.

First Edition
Published Internationally by Aussie Guys Books
ISBN: 978-1-7642115-4-3
All rights reserved worldwide.

Dedication

For the child I once was, who believed silence
meant unworthiness, who carried burdens too
heavy for small shoulders, who learned to
survive before he learned to speak.

For the man I became, who found the courage
to stay, to listen, to forgive, and to turn pain
into purpose.

For my children whose laughter rewrote my
story, whose love reminds me every day
that cycles can be broken, that gentleness
is strength, and that we are never
defined by where we begin.

And for every soul who has ever stood
at the edge of despair and chosen, somehow,
to take one more breath - this book is for you.

May you find in these pages what
I finally found in myself:

The light that stayed.

—William Power

"Are you my mother?
—*PD. Eastman*

Contents

Preface

This book began as a whisper I tried to ignore.

For years, I carried stories I told no one - not because I was ashamed, but because I didn't yet have the language to tell them without breaking. Silence was safer. It kept the memories folded, the feelings muted, the truth manageable. But silence, I've learned, doesn't forget. It waits. It speaks in the spaces between breaths, asking softly, What if you told the truth, and survived it?

This book is my answer to that question.

It isn't a story about blame or bitterness. It's a story about belonging - about what happens when you are bought, named, raised, loved, and broken by the same hands. It's a journey through the long echo of adoption, through the invisible scars left by narcissistic abuse, and through the fragile beauty of forgiveness. It's about the way pain, when faced with honesty, can become purpose.

I didn't write this book to accuse anyone. I wrote it to understand everyone - especially myself. I wanted to make peace with the people who shaped me, even the ones who hurt me most. I wanted to stand before my past and say, "Thank you for teaching me how to survive." Because survival, as it turns out, was only the first lesson. The real lesson was learning how to live.

The title We Bought YOU has haunted me since childhood - words that once felt like a sentence have become an invitation. They forced me to ask: what is the value of a life? What makes a family? What happens when love feels like a transaction, and how do we find worth beyond it? In searching for those answers, I found something far greater - the quiet truth that love is not possession; it is presence. It is staying, even when the world teaches you to run.

If you've picked up this book, perhaps you, too, are searching for that kind of peace. Perhaps you've known what it feels like to be unseen, unheard, or unloved in the way you needed. If so, I hope these pages remind you that you are not alone - and that your story, like mine, can still become something beautiful.

This is not the end of my story; it's only the beginning. It is the first light after a long night, the moment before forgiveness becomes freedom. There are more books to come, more reckonings, more grace. But everything starts here - with the truth, with the silence, and with the light that stayed.

Thank you for listening.

Thank you for being brave enough to read.

—Will

Introduction

Memory is a strange country. You think you've left it behind until a smell, a sound, a question pulls you back through the gates. For me, it began in a classroom, sunlight slanting across wooden desks, the sound of chalk scratching at the blackboard. Our teacher asked us to write about our first memory. Around me, pencils started moving, children whispering to each other about birthday cakes and family holidays, about first pets and Christmas mornings. But when I tried to remember, what came to me wasn't joy. It was a sentence.

"We bought you."

Those words have followed me my whole life. At the time, I didn't understand them, not the way adults do. I only knew how they felt, heavy, confusing, final. Like a price had been paid and somehow I owed something I couldn't name. I was too young to know what adoption meant, too old to ignore the tone it carried when my mother said it. Her voice was never soft, never reassuring. It was matter of fact, as though love was a contract, and I was the fine print.

I remember sitting at my desk, pencil hovering over the paper, realising that my first memory wasn't a picture, it was a feeling. The feeling of being owned. The room spun with laughter and chalk dust, but inside I was still hearing her voice, the way she said it like a fact she wanted the world to remember. "We bought you." I didn't know it then, but that moment would define how I saw everything that came after, family, faith, love, belonging.

We lived in a small country town where summers burned and winters bit hard, where everything seemed either endless or unreachable. The land itself was honest, it gave what it could, took what it needed, and didn't pretend to care. I think that's why I loved it. The dirt never lied. People did. At home, love was measured in obedience. Gratitude was a currency, and I was always overdrawn.

When I looked at my classmates writing their innocent memories, I envied them, not for their stories, but for their certainty. They belonged to someone without question. I belonged with an asterisk.

That was the first time I learned that truth doesn't always sound cruel when it's spoken; sometimes it sounds ordinary. And sometimes it comes disguised as love.

I didn't know then that those words, that memory, would one day become the title of this book. That they would be the seed of everything I'd spend a lifetime trying to understand. But in that moment, sitting in that classroom, the story had already begun. And so, this is where I'll begin too.

Part I — The Making of a Secret

Chapter 1

The Ghost Memory

We were told to write our first memory. The air in the classroom was thick with chalk dust and the hum of children who still believed that memories were supposed to be happy things. I remember the teacher smiling as she said it, her cardigan the colour of porridge, her voice soft and even like she was inviting us into something safe. Most of the kids bent their heads straight away, pencils scratching. Some were already whispering about birthdays, beaches, the smell of their grandmother's kitchen. I stared at the page for a long time before I wrote the only words that had ever been told to me about my beginning: "Mum and Dad bought me at a shop".

When the teacher leaned over my shoulder she paused, her breath catching just slightly before she smoothed her expression back into kindness. "That's very… honest, Will," she said, but her eyes flicked away like she'd seen something she shouldn't have. Then she moved on, and I sat there staring at the words, the way they looked smaller than they sounded at home.

At the age of eight, I didn't know there was another way for a story to start. I thought some children came from a shop, or at least that there was a place where families went to buy children who were missing. The sentence wasn't strange to me. It was law, like chores, or the way the sun always came up over the far paddock whether you were ready or not.

Our farm sat just outside a country town where summer burned everything to a crisp and winter bit at your fingers like punishment. The mornings smelled of hay, dust, and milk. When I was old enough to carry a bucket without spilling, I was old enough to be useful. Every day before school I would drag myself out to the dairy shed where the old brown cow waited, steaming in the cold. The stool creaked beneath me, the metal bucket filled with warmth, and for a few quiet minutes it felt like the world forgot to demand anything else from me. The cow shed was my first church, the rhythm of milk against the metal my first prayer.

Kylie would be in the kitchen by then, making lunches the way Mum liked them: sandwiches cut on the diagonal, crusts gone, cling wrap pulled tight enough to suffocate the bread. Kylie was eighteen months older and already had a voice like steel wrapped in velvet. She'd been adopted first, part of the doctor's plan to make our mother more "maternal," to awaken a body that refused to do what was expected of it. The doctor said sometimes holding a child made the womb remember what it was meant for. It must have worked, because not long after I arrived, the miracle babies came, first one, then another, two sons with her blood, her eyes, and her unshakable belief that they were proof she'd won some private war with God.

From the moment the first "blood boy" came, the rules in the house changed. Gratitude became a language Kylie, and I learned fluently. Blood meant belonging. Adoption meant debt. Love wasn't a gift; it was a transaction that never cleared.

Mum came from nothing, though she never admitted it. Dad told me once that the house they first moved into after marriage, had a dirt floor, that she used to sweep it every day just to feel clean. He said it softly, almost kindly, but she must have heard because later that night his voice turned to silence. Poverty was her original sin, and she spent the rest of her life atoning for it with polish and presentation. To her, money was proof of virtue, and poor people were moral failures. She wasn't cruel because she enjoyed it; she was cruel because she was terrified someone might see the dirt still clinging to her.

Dad was quieter. He worked the land; shoulders bent under weather and guilt. His hands were calloused, his eyes tired, but there was gentleness there, hidden under obedience. When she told him to discipline us, he did, but he never looked directly at me while he did it. He'd stand in the hallway after, the strap still in his hand, eyes shining with something he couldn't name. I think he hated her for needing it and hated himself for doing it.

Inside our house, everything was order and inspection. Floors shined, towels matched, windows gleamed. Outside, the land stretched wild, full of dust and noise and honesty. I learned early that the paddocks told no lies. The wind might scold, the sun might burn, but they never pretended to be anything other than what they were. I found comfort there, in the hum of insects, in the lowing of cattle, in the dirt under my fingernails that she called disgusting but that felt like truth to me.

Sometimes I'd stand at the fence line after chores, long after the sky had stopped pretending to be morning. From there, the land looked endless, the kind of endless that made you ache. The wire hummed with the wind, the posts leaned like old men keeping secrets, and I'd stare until the horizon blurred and I could almost imagine walking past it. I didn't yet have the word freedom, but I knew the feeling, like air waiting on the other side.

One afternoon, Kylie found me out there. She leaned against the fence beside me, her hair catching bits of sunlight.

"You know she only says it to make you feel small," she said.

"Who?" I asked, though I already knew.

"Mum. About being bought."

I kicked at the dirt. "She says it to you too."

Kylie smiled, but it didn't reach her eyes. "Yeah, but I'm the practice one. You're the investment."

I didn't know what that meant then, not really, but it sounded true in a way that made my stomach twist.

When I asked Mum about it once, she laughed, a brittle, sharp sound that didn't belong to happiness.

"Don't be silly," she said. "You should be grateful. We saved you."

That word, saved, carried more weight than I could bear. Saved from what? From whom? She never said. Gratitude was supposed to erase the question.

The farm demanded everything. Work was constant, rest a rumour. Before school I milked; after school I fed animals, weeded, raked, fixed fences. The strap hung by the kitchen door, silent most days but never forgotten. It was the punctuation mark on every conversation: Do as you're told, or else.

Still, there were moments when Dad and I found something like peace. Sometimes he'd meet me by the fence after dark. He'd switch off the ute and lean against the bonnet, both of us staring into the dark.

"Fence is straight," he'd say after a while.

I'd nod. He'd light his pipe, draw once, and offer it to me. I'd shake my head. He'd smile like that was the right answer. We didn't talk about home. Silence was safer.

Mum never joined us. She hated the smell of smoke and the sound of stillness. She said quiet people had something to hide. Maybe that's why she was always talking, filling the house with words that meant nothing but weighed everything down.

Kylie once told me that Mum was scared of being ordinary.

"She wants people to think we're rich," she said. "She thinks if she looks perfect long enough, she'll become it."

Kylie's voice carried both pity and defiance, like she already knew she'd never fit into Mum's version of a life. I wanted to tell her I felt the same, but the words stayed stuck behind my teeth, where all my words went back then.

I remember one night, sitting at the table after dinner, when Mum turned to me and said,

"You should be thankful, Will. Not everyone gets to be chosen."

Her smile was polished to perfection, but her eyes were measuring. "Imagine where you'd be if we hadn't taken you in."

I stared at my plate; at the peas I'd pushed into a line like soldiers. "I don't know," I said.

"That's right," she replied, satisfied. "You'd be nowhere."

It wasn't until much later that I realised nowhere was exactly where I longed to be, out past the fence line, beyond the reach of her voice, where I could disappear into the wind and maybe find out who I was when no one was looking.

The night before I turned eight, I woke to thunder. The air smelled of rain and earth and something like freedom. I crept outside, bare feet on cold boards, and walked until I reached the fence. Lightning flashed across the sky, silvering the paddocks, and for a second everything looked clean. I gripped the wire, the metal biting into my palms, and whispered into the wind, "One day."

The words slipped away into the darkness, but they stayed with me, coiling somewhere deep, a promise I didn't yet understand.

Chapter 2

Are You My Mother

Memory is a strange thing. It never sits still. It flickers like a mirage above a dirt road, solid but shimmering one second, gone the next. Sometimes it invents new details to make sense of old pain. My earliest real memory isn't of people at all; it's of a book.

The cover was worn smooth by other children's hands, the pages soft from use. Are You My Mother? - a story about a baby bird that falls from its nest and wanders the world asking everything it meets who it belongs to.

I remember sitting cross-legged on the classroom floor while the teacher read aloud, her voice bright and safe, and feeling a knot twist inside me. The other kids laughed when the bird asked a cow if she was his mother. I didn't. I wanted the cow to say yes. I wanted someone to say yes.

When the bell rang and everyone rushed out, I stayed behind, staring at the pictures. The bird finally finds his real mother, and they fly home together. I traced the drawing with my finger and thought how lucky he was that someone came back for him. At home that night I asked,

"Mum, do you know that story about the baby bird who looks for his mum?"

My mother didn't look up from folding tea towels.

"Children's nonsense," she said. "That poor bird should have been grateful anything found them at all."

Her words settled like dust in my lungs. Gratitude was her favourite lesson; it was also her favourite weapon. Whenever she talked about real mothers, she did it with the same tone she used for people who didn't polish their shoes.

Kylie once whispered that she'd heard Mum call our birth mothers foolish women who'd made stupid mistakes.

"She says we were rescued," Kylie told me, her eyes sharp with understanding too old for her age.

"But sometimes it feels like we were just trophies she didn't have to polish."

Our house was full of trophies - gleaming surfaces, measured curtains, everything arranged to look effortless. Nothing about it was effortless. Every towel had to hang evenly, every spoon face up, every answer rehearsed before guests came.

When she spoke to visitors, Mum's laugh was soft and expensive, but the minute the door closed it dropped away like a mask too tight to breathe behind. She'd turn to us and say,

"Don't slouch. People always notice."

She talked about money the way other mothers talked about faith - as something holy, proof you were chosen. Poor people, she always said, had no self-respect. I didn't understand how she could hate them when she'd been one of them.

Dad rarely corrected her due to what I believe was fear. My sister told me that dad attempted fate with addressing mum's attitude, just once.

"Who the fuck do you think you are... The queen". You can guess the outcome.

Apparently, mum ignored him for months after that, so, at times like these, he'd just nod and retreat to his shed outside, the smell of gunpowder, oil and metal swallowing him whole. Later I'd realise the shed was his sanctuary, his mancave, the only place he could exist without her script.

Spring was the hardest time. The paddocks filled with pollen, and I filled with sneezes. She hated weakness almost as much as she hated dust.

"Stop sniffling," she'd snap while polishing a row of glass ornaments.

"You sound common."

I learned to hold my breath until the tickle passed, eyes watering, chest tight. Even my allergies felt like disobedience.

Kylie and I used to sit under the apricot tree behind the house when the light turned honey-gold and talk about what it would be like to have a mother who laughed.

"Maybe our real ones do," she'd say. "Maybe they laugh all the time."

I wanted to believe that. I pictured a woman who smelled of soap and bread, who didn't care if your shoes were dirty as long as you were happy. A ghost mother who lived in the spaces between chores, waiting for me to remember her.

One day, after Mum had spent the afternoon comparing herself to some woman in town - richer, prettier, but "without taste" - she looked straight at me and said,

"You should remember how lucky you are. Some children never get to live in a real home."

I didn't know what to say, so I said thank you, because that was the only safe answer.

She smiled then, the way cats do when the mouse finally stops running.

That night I couldn't sleep. The house creaked like it was trying to speak. I stared at the ceiling and thought about the bird again, about how he'd asked every creature he met if they were his mother. I wondered what would happen if he never found her. Would he keep asking forever? Would he stop believing she existed? Or would he decide that maybe he didn't need a mother at all? That thought scared me more than any beating ever had, because it felt too close to what I was already becoming.

Years later, when people asked me what my childhood was like, I'd tell them about the farm - the cows, the wheat, the heat - but never about the book. It's easier to talk about work than longing. Work has edges; longing is endless. Still, whenever I saw a bird struggling against the wind, I'd find myself whispering, "are you my mother?" and waiting for an answer that never came.

Chapter 3

Rules, Belts & Silence

The house had its own heartbeat, and it thudded in time with her footsteps. Mornings began before the sun, not with birdsong but with commands.

"Up. Beds made and shoes clean." The words landed like stones, small and relentless.

I used to think the house itself was afraid of her; even the walls seemed to hold their breath when she entered a room.

The strap always hung beside the kitchen door, always in sight, and polished by the years of being handled more than used. It was less of a tool than a threat, a reminder that perfection had a price. Dad oiled it sometimes, his hands careful, reverent almost as though he was tending a relic rather than a weapon. He never met my eyes when he did it.

"Rules keep order," he'd mutter.

Not to me but to the air, and I'd nod because nodding was safer than asking what kind of order required fear to stay alive.

Kylie never nodded. She had a spark that refused to dim, a tilt of her chin that made Mum's lips tighten.

"Answer when you're spoken to," Mum would say, and Kylie would, just not the way she expected.

There was a kind of poetry in my sister's defiance. It felt soft, almost musical, but every verse ended the same way: with silence and the soft click of a buckle being unhooked from its mounting. Afterward, Mum would pour herself a very weak tea and hum, satisfied that the universe was back in line.

Outside, the paddocks didn't care who ruled. The wind still pushed through the wheat, the cows still lowed for feed, the sun still climbed and burned and fell. I'd lose myself in that rhythm, in the honesty of things that didn't lie. The animals never demanded gratitude. They only wanted care, and in giving it I felt, for a while, like someone worth saving.

The kitchen smelled of polish and boiled vegetables, the kind of smell that clung to everything, shirts, curtains, even sleep. Mum moved through it like a general inspecting the troops, her fingers trailing over counters, eyes searching for proof that we had failed her. Every evening was a test we hadn't studied for.

"Did you sweep the porch?"

"Did you wipe the prints from the glass?"

If the answer came too slow, the strap would twitch on its hook, reminding us to speak quickly and clearly. Gratitude first, explanation never.

Dad usually came in from the paddocks at dusk, the weight of the day still hanging from his shoulders. He'd stand in the doorway for a brief moment, pipe and hat in hand, before stepping into her world of order.

She'd look him over the way she looked at everything, assessing value.

"Go and wash up," she'd say, and he always did. Not that he needed to be reminded daily.

At the table he was quiet, except for his loud chewing from his poorly fitted dentures. His eyes on his plate. If we spoke out of turn, he'd clear his throat once. That was warning enough.

"Let's have no fuss tonight," he would murmur, which meant be invisible.

I think he believed silence could protect us, the way wire protects a paddock, keep the danger in one place. He never saw that it also kept us fenced inside it.

Kylie tested every boundary. She would hum under her breath while she dried the dishes, or answer a ridiculous question with another of equal value just to feel the shape of defiance on her tongue. I admired her for it even when it scared me.

One night she said, "She can't hit us both if we stick together."

Her whisper carried the tremor of someone who wasn't sure she was right. I wanted to believe her, but the house taught a different lesson.

The next morning Mum found the stack of dishes uneven. "Who did this?" she demanded.

Kylie stepped forward before I could. The strap came down once, twice, the sound sharp and final. Mum's breathing slowed afterward, like pain had soothed her.

"Maybe now you'll remember," she said.

I did. I remembered everything.

Work filled the spaces between those moments. Before school I hauled feed for the animals, after school I weeded, raked, mowed and gardened until the light went grey. My hands grew calloused, my body small but strong. Sometimes I wondered if that was the point, to build me into a tool she could use, like the mower or the rake, dependable and silent.

When neighbours visited, she instantly waved from the gate. She'd lift her hand symbolic of royalty, her smile perfect and her voice sweet. To them we were the picture of diligence: the proud mother, the obedient children, the quiet husband. It was a lie polished as bright as the windows.

At night, when the house finally slept, I'd lie awake counting the seconds between the ticks of the clock. I told myself that if I could keep the rhythm steady, the world would stay steady too. I didn't yet know the word trauma; I only knew the feeling of waiting for something to break. Even dreams came in whispers, Kylie's laugh carried on the wind, the fence line glowing faintly under moonlight, a voice that might have been my own saying, "hold on".

Sometimes Dad would find me in the shed, pretending to fix something. He'd stand beside me, hands in pockets.

"You workin' hard?" he'd ask, and I'd nod.

"Good. Keep busy. It helps."

He meant it kindly, but busyness was just another kind of silence. Still, I liked those moments. He didn't ask questions he didn't want answers to, and I didn't give him any.

We existed side by side, two ghosts haunting the same house in different ways.

The strap didn't leave marks you could see for long, but the sound of it stayed. It hummed in my ears even when it wasn't moving, like an echo that refused to fade. I started to measure time by it, the spaces between punishments, the small reprieves of calm.

When weeks passed without the sound, hope would rise like sap after rain. Then a mistake, a spill, a word said wrong, and it would all return. Afterward Mum would smooth her hair, tell me she only wanted the best for me.

"Discipline builds character," she'd say.

I'd nod because I'd learned the trick of it: agree fast, breathe shallow, wait for the moment to end.

What she never saw, what none of them did, was that every rule she set built not character but distance. Each demand, each order, pushed me further toward the fields, toward the quiet that didn't hurt. The land was rough, but it was honest. It never asked for gratitude. Out there I could pretend the wind was a voice older than hers, telling me to keep walking.

I didn't yet understand that the silence I was learning would follow me long after I left, that it would shape the way I loved, the way I fought, the way I forgave. Back then it was just survival, a thin thread between the boy I was and the boy who wanted to be free.

When the house finally settled each night, boards creaking like old bones, I'd whisper to the dark, "One day," the same words I'd spoken to the fence line. The promise stayed small but alive, pulsing like a second heartbeat under my skin.

Kylie started keeping a notebook. It was small, light blue, the kind that used to hold spelling lists. She wrote in it late at night, the torch beam hidden under the quilt. I didn't know what she wrote, only that she guarded it like a secret map. "It helps," she said once.

"When I write it down, it can't take over me."

I didn't understand then that she was giving me the blueprint for survival. Years later, when I began to write my own words, I realised she had planted that seed in the dark.

Our pact was simple: if one of us got caught in her storm, the other stayed silent. Not out of cowardice, but because speaking only fed the fire. We learned the rhythm of her moods, the way the air changed before the lightning struck. On good days, she'd hum while polishing silver; on bad ones, the hum vanished and the whole house leaned into dread. Those were the days when Dad moved slower, softer, as if hoping the air might forget him. When it didn't, he'd reach for the strap, eyes already defeated.

"You know I have to," he'd whisper.

I wanted to ask who had told him that, but I was afraid he didn't know the answer himself.

The more she demanded perfection, the more we retreated to the margins of the property. The fruit trees behind the shed became our refuge. We'd sit there in the branches after our chores were all done, sap sticking to our hands, talking about faraway places neither of us had seen.

"One day," Kylie said, "I'll have a house with walls that don't echo." I asked what she meant.

"These ones throw everything back at you," she said.

I looked at the house, at its crooked external lines, its sun scorched weatherboard cladding and realised she was right. Even silence bounced off those walls, louder than shouting.

When the first frost came, the mornings turned white and brittle. Mum complained that we tracked mud inside, that our breath fogged the windows she'd just polished.

"Ungrateful," she muttered as she scrubbed.

The word slid off her tongue so easily it sounded like a name. Maybe that's what we were to her, a reminder of everything she thought she'd risen above.

The night that changed everything was quiet to begin with. The air was heavy, the sky a lid of cloud. She'd been in one of her cleaning frenzies, chasing specks of dust that no one else could see. A vase slipped from her hand and shattered. I flinched at the sound; she turned on me instantly.

"Look what you made me do!" she shouted.

I hadn't moved, but truth didn't matter. Kylie stepped between us before I could speak.

"It's just a vase," she said. "You have others."

The silence that followed was thick enough to drown in. Mum's face went still, too still, then she reached for it. The sound that came next wasn't loud, but it filled every corner of me. Afterward, Kylie's breath came in short, ragged bursts, and I knew she was counting them to prove she was still here.

Later, when the house slept, I crept to her room. She was sitting on the floor, notebook open, pencil moving slowly. I sat beside her without speaking. She turned a page and pushed it toward me. We're not crazy, she'd written. We're just trapped. I nodded. It felt like the first honest sentence I'd ever read.

After that night, something in me settled into watchfulness. I learned how to read moods the way farmers read the sky. I became fluent in danger's dialect, the hitch of breath, the tremor in a voice, the silence that meant run. I didn't know then that these skills would follow me into every room of my adult life, that I'd spend years mistaking vigilance for love. Back then it was just survival.

When I think of that time now, what surprises me most isn't the fear but the small, stubborn hope threaded through it. Hope was the sound of Kylie's pencil on paper, the feel of cold air before dawn, the fence line waiting at the edge of the property. Hope was the quiet promise we made to each other: that we would get out, that the world beyond those paddocks was real, that one day the word "home" might mean something gentle.

Chapter 4

My Sister and the Mirror

In the winter Kylie turned fourteen, the frost came early and stayed. It glazed the paddocks silver before dawn, crisping the grass so that every step cracked like glass. We woke each morning in a fog of our own breath and the smell of damp woollen blankets. Mum hated winter because she couldn't keep the windows open; the house felt smaller when the cold shut us in together. She prowled from room to room, rearranging, perfecting, like order could keep the temperature from falling. Kylie said it was the season when even the mirrors shivered.

The mirror in the hallway was mum's favourite, tall, gold-framed, spotless. She'd stand in front of it adjusting the line of her outfit, the tilt of her hair, her mouth forming the smile she used for visitors. I used to watch from the doorway, wondering what she saw when she looked at herself for so long. Once, when she caught me staring, she said,

"Presentation is everything. People only respect what looks respectable."

Then she looked past me, into the mirror again, and added, "Remember that."

I did. I just didn't know which part she wanted me to remember, the respect or the reflection.

Kylie started using that same mirror differently. When Mum wasn't around, she'd pull faces at it, twist her mouth, cross her eyes until she dissolved into laughter.

"She can't have what she can't control," she whispered.

I wanted to believe it. Watching her made the fear thin out a little, like a fog burning off. But it never lasted. Mum always seemed to sense laughter; it drew her like a challenge.

She'd appear suddenly in the doorway, smile fixed, voice sweet.

"What's so funny?" And just like that, the air would change.

That year brought the first real crack in the house's facade. Mum was distracted, sick some mornings, angry others. The doctor's car came up the drive more often. Kylie said she'd heard them talking in the kitchen about "miracles" and "timing." When the truth of the impending pregnancy was revealed, mum's pride swelled like the belly that followed. She moved through the house radiant and sharp-edged, a queen whose power had been confirmed.

"At last," she said to Dad loud enough for us to hear, "a child of my own blood."

The words fell heavy, but I didn't yet understand how deep they'd cut.

Kylie did. She stopped using the mirror after that.

"No point looking," she said. "We'll never be what she really wants to see."

I told her she was wrong, that one day things would change, but the look she gave me said she'd already stopped believing in change that came from inside these walls. We spent more time outside, hiding in the orchard or under the apricot tree, talking about the world beyond the hills.

"When I go," she said, "I'm taking that mirror with me. I'll hang it somewhere the sun hits it first thing in the morning, so it can finally show something nice."

I laughed, but the image stuck, the mirror catching real light, not just the kind she polished into it.

As Mum's stomach grew, so did her need for perfection. Every speck of dust became an insult, every mistake a threat to her new image of motherhood. The strap always visible, the warning bell that never stopped ringing.

The night before the baby came, the whole house smelled of disinfectant and rain. Mum paced the hallway, one hand on her back, the other brushing the mirror's frame.

"Everything must look right," she said.

"Everything." I wanted to ask her for whom, but I didn't. Some questions were just new ways to get hurt.

When the baby arrived, the house filled with visitors and flowers. Everyone said she was glowing. She was. It was the glow of victory. Kylie and I stood at the edge of the crowd, smiling because that's what we'd been trained to do.

Later, after the last car left, Mum turned to us and said,

"Now you have a brother. You'll have to help me, of course."

Her tone made it sound like a mandate. That night I watched her hold him, feed him, the only time I'd ever seen her touch something gently. The sight made my stomach twist inside, not jealousy exactly, but the ache of watching a kindness you knew wasn't meant for you.

Kylie whispered, "She finally got the thing she wanted. Look at him, he looks just like her."

I wanted to cover my ears, not because it wasn't true, but because it was. From then on the baby was proof that blood meant worth. We were the shadows cast by his light. The mirror belonged to her again, and she never stopped looking.

Even our relatives could see it. The quiet hierarchy that settled over the family like dust no one wanted to disturb. They'd smile and say how blessed she was, how the little one was her "true reflection." I'd stand beside Kylie, both of us wearing our practiced smiles, hearing the unspoken part: that we were borrowed blessings, substitutes until nature delivered the real thing.

No one said it outright, but we felt it in every pat on his head, every comparison disguised as praise. The golden child wasn't just her favourite. He became the family's proof that she had finally succeeded. And from that day forward, the rest of us were measured against him and found wanting.

Just three years later, another blood heir.

Chapter 5

Sunday and Other Tests

Sundays were supposed to be the softest day of the week, a sigh after six days of being useful, but in our house, they were duties with hymns. She did not come with us; she never did. She stood at the doorway like a foreman, checking hair and hems, the shine on our shoes, the angle of a parting, breathing out rules and warnings as if we were marching to war.

"Sit straight. Speak when spoken to. Make me a proud mother."

Proud meant invisible. Proud meant no one noticed the seam that had split, the bruise that wouldn't quite disappear, the way fear made your spine remember to be a ruler.

Then she would close the door behind us and the house would keep her for itself.

On Sundays, Dad would drive us to the Presbyterian church for mass and then all the children would attend Sunday school lessons. He'd pull up at the same corner each week, not in front, but just around the bend, out of sight from the congregation. We'd climb out, straighten our clothes, and walk the short distance alone, pretending it was normal. Our full blood siblings were much to young to attend.

The church sat on a small but deliberate rise like something planted to be admired. Deep stone walls, stained glass windows, and a bell that pretended it rang for God and not for order. We slipped into the right pew because there was only ever one right place to sit, and we made our faces quiet. I liked the first moments best, before the organ remembered to be loud, when everyone whispered and shuffled and the light had not yet chosen who to bless. I would count the slats in the ceiling, the knots in the timber, the paths the dust took in the sun; if I counted steadily enough my chest forgot to tighten. Kylie leaned close once and breathed,

"It's only an hour," and even that sounded like hope.

People in town loved our family, or at least the version of it that nodded and sang in time. They loved the idea of a woman so devoted she sent her children to church every week, spotless and obedient. They loved the way we said please and yes and thank you for the sermon. They would take my hand on the steps and say,

"Tell your mother what a credit you are," and I would say I would.

In the end they would go home satisfied that goodness was the same as polish. After all, cleanliness was close to godliness in our mothers eyes.

Sometimes there was a wedding, flowers and rice and a bride who didn't know yet that congratulations can be as heavy as a ball and chain, and she would appear then, elegant as a photograph, prayer hands being offered, a careful smile, the kind of woman who was never poor except in memory.

She stood for a quality baptism too, and funerals of reputable locals to showcase that these the big days proved a life was worth noticing.

People said she had such dignity. People said she must be so proud. She would tilt her head just enough to agree.

Inside the service I learned how to pass as peaceful. When the minister lifted his arms too quickly, my shoulders rose before I could stop them. When the organist hit a sour note I felt it like a door slamming. I sat with my hands pressed flat to my thighs and tried to keep my breath small so the panic would not hear it and come running.

The stories were good ones, forgiveness like fresh water, mercy for the lost, the last sheep carried home, but I kept waiting for what came after the stories, the part where the strap is waiting by the pantry door for anyone who forgets the rules. No one preached that part. I learned it elsewhere.

After the last hymn the air outside felt like relief even when it was hot enough to bend the horizon. The elders stood in a row like fence, the posts admiring themselves: how straight, how sound. They took turns telling us we were models of discipline and how lucky we were, and I said thank you because thank you was the currency that bought safety. Kylie said thank you too, but her eyes went hard the way a sky goes before weather. She had started to keep a tiny notebook even on Sundays, pretending it was a prayer list. I knew better. Prayer asks; notes remember. She was keeping our life somewhere it couldn't be polished away.

When there were no ceremonies to draw her, mum spent Sundays at home staging a life. She ironed linen that no one used, arranged roses in vases we weren't allowed to be touch, moved a chair two inches left and called it vision. Sometimes neighbours came by with sponge cake and gossip, and she would accept both, say how terribly rushed she was, how difficult it was to manage four children, how important it was to keep standards in a world where people let everything slide. They would nod because anyone who sounds certain is easy to believe.

If they asked why she didn't come to church herself she would smile like a secret and say she preferred to keep her devotion private, and they would agree that modesty was the most elegant kind of faith. I wanted to tell them that faith wasn't modesty at all, it was a body remembering how to breathe when the room went small, but I didn't. I had learned the survival value of silence, the way it can wear a halo if you hold it still enough.

There was a Sunday in late spring when the gum trees in town were all flowering, and the heat had charged the air with the scent of eucalyptus. The sermon was steeped in tradition, about the splendour of the white cockatoo and the radiance of the golden yellow sunflower. The way they never worry, and all I could think was that cockatoos don't have mothers who measure them, and sunflowers don't get told to polish their leaves until they shine or suffer the wrath that follows.

On the steps the minister shook my hand so firmly I felt the bones speaking to one another.

"Your mother's a marvel," he said. "What great discipline, and fantastic standards she has given you."

"Yes, sir," I said, and wondered how good a lie has to be before it becomes a truth. We would carry that lie home with the hymn still stuck in our heads.

When Sunday school lessons ended, we'd find dad waiting in the same place, engine running, eyes fixed on the road. He never came around the corner. You see, Dad was a non-practicing Catholic, baptized as a baby by his loving parents and raised in the Christian faith. But we never saw that at home. Never. Whatever faith he had, lived quietly inside him, hidden behind the same silences that ruled our house.

Mum always would meet us at the door with a cloth in one hand and a complaint in the other. This time it would be,

"Boot prints on the porch," she said, "and I suppose we'll have to eat early because some of us can't keep time."

I knew by the way the words lined up what the evening would cost.

The tests didn't end at the door. Sundays also came with a list. Did we set the table properly? Are the heavy forks on the outside, and the spoons shining as if they were trying to become something more than spoons? Did we fold the napkins like sails; did we eat with small mouths and perfect gratitude? There were questions to answer that were not questions.

"You understand how lucky you are?"

"Yes."

"You know what people think of this family?"

"Yes."

"You won't embarrass me?"

"No, I mean, yes."

The strap didn't need to appear to be part of the conversation. It lived in the grammar.

It was during one of those quiet Sunday dinners that she announced the future as if it were a platter she was bringing to the table. She had been reading a magazine about modern living, rooms with sharp corners and no dust, houses with windows that made the sky behave.

"We're selling," she said, like saying we were breathing.

"This," with a glance that took in the walls, the floor, our history "… is not who we are anymore."

She wanted a new build: brick and tile, clean lines, carpet and polished floors that did not remember footprints.

"Near town but not in it," she added, because one must be admired without being common.

"Plenty of land for a proper garden."

Garden meant work you could see from the road. I watched Dad's face for any sign of confirmation and saw what I always saw, a portal he wanted to pass through. He said,

"Your mum and I think that's best," and the decision became the next commandment we would keep.

I should say that some Sunday's were almost kind. There were afternoons when clouds shouldered the heat from the paddocks and the light fell gentle through the fruit trees and dad dosed off intermittently in a rocking chair with a whisky in one hand and his pipe in the other, and she forgot to find fault for a whole hour or more.

Those were the days I learned that kindness can be more dangerous than cruelty because it teaches you to hope. I would take that gift of time and spend it like money: a book, a lie-down, a walk to the fence line to see if the world had come any closer. It never did, but some days it looked like it might.

The first time a stranger noticed something true, it happened because of a laugh. After the church service a visiting woman from another town stopped me and said,

"You look like you're listening for thunder on a clear day."

She didn't say it unkindly. It startled me anyway; I didn't know you could see vigilance from the outside. She pressed a wrapped sweet into my palm like it was taboo and casually walked away. I didn't eat it. I kept it for weeks; sure, it meant something I wasn't ready to understand. Kylie said,

"Some people see right through glass," and I nodded and pretended we were made of brick.

As the plan to sell up and move grew legs, so did the work. A house shows better when it pretends no one has ever lived there. We scrubbed the skirting boards until our knuckles protested, pulled every weed as if it had cursed at her personally, whirled the mower over the yard until the lines in the grass looked military. Prospective buyers came, walked slow and careful and said how charming, how tidy, how modern it might be once someone did this or that. She smiled like a proprietor who had just closed a deal. After they drove away, she found something out of place and put it back with a sigh that meant we should have known without being told. I began to understand that we were walking exhibits. We performed the idea of family for strangers and looked to her afterward to see if the grade was a pass.

Sundays now bled into the rest of the week, and the rest of the week bled back into Sunday. That is what happens when your moral code is slavery. I learned to keep my shoulder blades flat, to make my voice a level line, to fold myself into the size of a boy who could pass for good. If I passed for long enough, I could make it through the door of the new house without a scene. That became the test: "Lord deliver us", to the next life without proof that the old one existed. We were remarkable at not existing.

It is also true that the body keeps its own ledger. On Sunday's I woke with a buzzing in my chest, a quiet hum that told me to map my exits and count my breaths. I learned to anchor myself with small, private rituals. Touch the hymnbook spine three times. Keep my thumb on the groove of the pew in front. Trace the pattern in the stained glass and call each colour by its name, slowly. It worked sometimes. Other times I would step outside mid-sermon and stand behind the hall where the bins gathered, where no one asked if I was blessed. The air back there smelled of oranges left too long in a bag and the sweet, rotten tang of flowers taken off the altar. I breathed that smell like medicine. When I could, I came back and made my face civil.

The last Sunday before the sale went through, the minister talked about houses on sand and houses on rock and what remains standing when the storm is over. It sounded like a riddle with only one wrong answer.

After the last amen, I stood on the steps and looked at the sky and pretended I could read it. I could not. But I could read my mother's eyes when we got home, the calculation there, and I could read my father's hands, the way they opened and closed like he was practicing letting go.

That afternoon she made us set the table twice for no reason I could find, then decided we would all go for a drive. We drove past houses that wore their money on their faces, and she pointed at one with a hedge cut like a soldier's jaw and said, "That's the one," and the car fell quiet around the word as if even the engine knew it had been given its orders.

I would like to tell you I prayed that night for a different house, that I asked any god who was listening to give us something smaller and kinder, but the truth is I did not pray. I lay awake and counted the seconds and made the promise I always made when I wanted to live long enough to see whether the world could change its mind. "One day". The words had been with me so long they no longer sounded like language. They sounded like breathing.

In the morning, we woke to a sky the colour of tin and a wind that got its fingers under the doors. She was already dressed when we came to the kitchen, lipstick perfect for a day no one would see.

"Up," she said, though we were, "and mind yourselves."

She pushed a pen and a sheet of paper toward me as if it were nothing.

"Write a list of what must be done before the agent comes."

I wrote sweep, polish, weed, smile. I did not write endure. I did not write survive. Those weren't chores in our house. Those were sacraments, and you didn't put sacraments on paper.

That was the Sunday I understood what tests are for. Not to measure progress but to teach endurance. The church taught it with parables, and we learned it with cutlery and garden implements. Between the two I began to grow the kind of quiet that passes for maturity when you are small. It is not maturity. It is weathering. It is waiting without breaking. It is the practice that lets you carry your childhood forward without spilling it in the foyer where people could slip and sue.

We sold within the month. Everyone said it was a sign. Mum said it was proof. Dad said it was quick. Kylie said nothing. I went to the fence line for what I didn't know then would be the last Sunday as it had always been and pressed my forehead to the timber rail and let the wind tell me what I could not tell myself.

The paddocks laid out like pages that didn't belong to me anymore. Somewhere beyond the far dam a bird called for nothing in particular and got an answer anyway. I wanted that kind of call, that kind of answer.

I stayed until my skin went cold and my breath made its own clouds, and I whispered the words that had become my spine. "One day". And then I went in to set the table the way she liked it, because sometimes, survival is doing the thing you hate with such precision, that no one can see the part of you already leaving.

Chapter 6

The Fence Line

The day we left the farm the wind ran ahead of us like a dog that didn't want to be kept. Dust rose behind the family station wagon in long brown sentences that said everything we weren't allowed to, goodbye, good riddance, we're still here.

She sat in the front calling out instructions to no one while dad watched the car's mirrors as if they were going to offer him an easier road if he stared long enough, hard enough.

Kylie and I rode in silence, measuring distance in fence posts and the way the horizon kept pretending to be nearby. I thought moving would feel like waking;

instead, it felt like remembering a dream you can't change.

The new place wasn't in town but it was close enough to smell it. A long, neat entrance driveway through a gate that locked with a sound that meant property, not welcome. Brick and tile, angles clean enough to slice, windows that made the sky behave. Inside, the rooms were almost bare, carpet new, curtains stiff, furniture pared back to the pieces that best explained we were now the kind of people who owned new things.

Outside, the land spread wider than any yard I'd ever seen. Not paddocks exactly, but an estate cut to be admired from the road, with acres of lawn, fruit trees in soldier-straight ranks, roses already plotting their way up trellises, garden beds edged so sharply they looked as if drawn with a ruler. She walked the perimeter once, chin high, taking inventory of a lifestyle she could now parade.

"This," she said, and her voice placed the flag. "This is who we are."

I was turning thirteen, old enough to know that a bigger stage doesn't change the play.

The work just changed costumes. Both the milking cow and chickens from the farm came with us, proof we were still practical under all that polish, and every morning before school I went out while the light was still deciding what kind of day it would be, my breath steaming, hands learning again the old rhythm of relief. The rest of the time belonged to grass and growth.

The mower and lawn edging tools waited like patient animals tucked away in the small garden shed. I had been introduced to them at the tender age of seven, my initiation into the family's belief that children should be useful, or not at all. And now their handles fit my grip, like they had been made to measure.

Up and back, up and back, lines straight enough to please a pilot. The scent of cut grass was rose sweet and heavy, and got into everything: hair, socks, the spaces behind my eyes. Roses needed pruning and had to be tied, the aphids scolded into obedience. Fruit trees needed spraying with toxic pesticides and given relentless manicures with a skill that felt like violence.

Plants wanted just one thing, but our mother wanted another. I was the difference.

For the first time we had neighbours close enough to hear laughter, or what passed for it. A couple to the left with twin boys and a little girl who rode her bike like she was learning to fly. A retired shearer to the right who waved with two fingers off the steering wheel, slow and friendly. The first week he came across with jars of home-made strawberry jam, some lemons and a joke about my mowing lines, how a plane could land on them in a storm. She laughed and told him she insisted on high standards, then she turned to me and said,

"You hear that? Keep them straight," as if the joke had been a directive that needed obeying.

Dad had obviously claimed the biggest of the two sheds and made it a place where the noise from the house couldn't find him. He called it a workshop, but everyone knows a mancave when they see one. He hung tools along the wall like a proud tradesman and securely anchored his gun safe to the floor in along the main wall. A poorly tuned and dented radio played songs older than we were and a fridge sat soundless in the corner filled with ginger ale and the kind of beer that forgives a man for saying nothing.

Sometimes dad would give me a task that took exactly as long as the silence we both needed. Whether reloading ammunition for the inevitable father and son duck hunting season or fixing something that really didn't need repair, we chose to spend time together.

"Be careful. A sharp edge needed here," he'd say, passing me a file, and we'd pretend the metal required our full attention.

Outside, she would stand and call through the thin shield of the metal door,

"Don't hide out here all day; there's work to be done," and then, the magic would lift.

He always said, "Just finishing," and wiped his hands on a rag like an apology.

School began a week after the last of the moving boxes were cleared from the living room. The bus came along the new estate road, and I learned the names of streets that sounded like they were trying too hard. The new year meant a new school for me and the uniform felt strange against a body that had been built for chores.

The first morning a teacher smiled and shook my hand and said,

"You'll love high school, fresh start!"

I wanted to tell him that you can't start fresh when the old story is stitched to your skin. Instead I smiled the way you do when people offer you hope they can't deliver.

At home, after school was out for the day, meant things were more urgent. The agent might still drive other buyer's past to admire what he had placed in the local paper under words like immaculate and commanding presence.

She didn't go to services, she kept her sabbath by polishing the world into the shape of her fear. If she heard laughter from over the hedge, she smiled without showing teeth and said,

"Some people have too much time," and then made another list.

By evening, the smell of polish and home cultivated floral arrangements would mingle through the house like proof of her devotion. Everything gleamed, even the things that were already clean. I'd watch her from the window, sleeves rolled, face set, remaking the world one surface at a time. Dad would be in the shed, the radio low, and the distance between them would hum like another kind of fence.

When the sun went down, the house grew quiet but never peaceful. The clocks ticked in rhythm with her footsteps. Even time seemed trained. I learned to move through rooms like a shadow. Seen, but not heard, useful but not belonging.

Out past the hedge, the neighbour's lights would flicker on, squares of gold across the lawn, ordinary life shining from just far enough away. Sometimes I'd stand at my window, breathing against the glass until it fogged, drawing small shapes in the mist before wiping them away.

It wasn't home yet. It was a display; a story told to the street. But somewhere beneath the trimmed roses and the lines of mown grass, something inside me had started listening, to the wind, to the silence, to the faint hum of the fence line that never stopped reminding me there was still a world beyond her lists.

Chapter 7

The Quiet Between Heartbeats

One Christmas after we had moved within the town limits, Santa Claus gifted me a stock whip. It was a bizarre gift; one I hadn't asked for and didn't know how to use. We didn't have cattle anymore, and I had never expressed an interest in owning a whip, but there it was, thirteen feet of braided leather with a hickory handle and a bound leather grip guard. I remember wondering why I'd been given this piece of craftsmanship, and on one fateful afternoon, I found out why the familiar strap was now missing.

I had been defiant toward my mother. Dad had been away for several days, and the details of the incident are vague at best, but I vividly remember running scared from her as she wielded the whip.

She lashed out at me, and the end of the whip caught me just below the chin. The last twelve inches, designed to inflict the most pain, wrapped around my neck and pulled me up short as she held the stock firm. The burning sting of the leather against my skin and the shock of being pulled back so abruptly was excruciating. The injury was severe, enough to leave a welt that encircled my neck, and I now know that a neighbour witnessed the incident and reported it to the authorities, though I was unaware of this at the time.

Later that night, as I stood in the mancave, the welt was still fresh, a physical reminder of the emotional pain I couldn't process. No means to hide the injury, it was there, in plain sight. The bruising had started, but the real scars were the ones I carried inside.

That night, after the dishes were packed away and my mother was bathing my youngest brother, I knew. I knew I couldn't do it anymore. The weight of the trauma was too much. Alone and desperate, I walked into my dad's shed of solitude, found the security keys, and unlocked the gun case. Inside was my rifle, front and centre and glaring back at me.

It felt right somehow, just to pick it up and to hold it. I loved that rifle. It had claimed many a rabbit in my solitary walks in the bushland that was our property. One hundred acres of trees and animals on the fringe of the town. It was heavy, solid, reliable, everything I felt I wasn't in that moment. I opened the cartridge drawer, searching for a .22 calibre bullet. I just needed one, but to my frustration, I couldn't find any. My dad always had bullets, plenty of them. There were bullets for all the other rifles, some were huge, capable of bringing down the largest of animals, but there were none for mine.

I looked for what felt like an eternity, rifling through the drawers, growing more desperate with each passing second. But nothing. Not a single bullet for my rifle. What the hell!

I paused, and in that moment, something shifted inside me. I felt different, though I couldn't explain why. With the rifle still firmly gripped in my hands, I closed the breach, pointed the empty barrel at my temple and pulled the trigger.

The click was deafening, as though the entire world had gone silent, leaving only that hollow sound reverberating in my ears. I stood there, frozen, staring down the empty barrel of my rifle. The realization of what had just happened hit me like a wave. I had pulled the trigger. It should have been over. But it wasn't.

My mind raced to make sense of it. Why weren't there any bullets? How could that be? There had always been bullets. I had seen them in that drawer many times before. My dad was meticulous about keeping his supplies in order, making sure everything was in its proper place. And yet, on the one night when I needed those bullets, when I was ready to end it all, they were nowhere to be found.

I was dumbfounded. Confused. And in that confusion, a strange feeling began to take root in my chest, something that felt entirely foreign in that moment of darkness. I couldn't explain it at the time, but it was as if the universe had intervened. It was as if some unseen force had decided that tonight wasn't my night. That I wasn't meant to go through with it. That I was supposed to stay.

I locked the rifle back in the cupboard, my hands shaking as I fumbled with the key. It felt surreal, like I was watching someone else perform the motions of locking it away. The night air outside was cool, but inside, I felt nothing but cold. I was numb.

I walked back into the house, where life went on as usual. My mother was still bathing my brother, and everything was as it had been. No one had the slightest idea of what had just happened. No one knew how close I had come to disappearing from their lives forever.

Obviously, I didn't sleep much that night. My mind was consumed with questions. How? Why? How had this happened? Was it just a coincidence that I couldn't find the bullets? Or was it something more? Was it a sign, a message that I wasn't ready to understand?

At the time, I didn't have the emotional tools to process it, but something deep inside told me that this night was far more significant than I could grasp.

In the morning I woke up early, long before the rest of the house had stirred. I was drawn back to the mancave, almost like I needed to return to the scene of the crime, to make sense of it. I crept outside, my heart pounding in my chest as I approached the door. It felt strange to be doing this in the daylight, with the sun just starting to rise. The whole world looked different, but I felt the same weight of the previous night still pressing on my shoulders. The smell of peach blossoms was heavy in the air, and the dew from the cold night was hanging from the clothesline as the birds were calling their morning song to welcome in the day. Is this for real?

I unlocked the cupboard again and opened the drawer, just as I had done the night before. And there, sitting in plain sight, was the box of ammunition I had been desperately looking for. The box of .22 calibre bullets, neatly tucked away, exactly where it should have been. Three boxes in fact, neatly stacked and smirking at me as I gazed upon them. Two more magazines filled to the brim with ammunition laying just to the left.

I went cold. My hands shook as I stared once more at my fate. How was this possible? I had searched that drawer for what felt like forever, and it had been fruitless. I was certain of it. I hadn't just missed them. They weren't there. And yet, here they are, as though they had re-appeared overnight.

My breath caught in my throat, and I felt the weight of something larger than myself pressing down on me. I couldn't explain it, but I knew in that moment that something had intervened. Something had stopped me from finding those bullets when I believed I needed them most. I couldn't shake the feeling. Had I just witnessed a miracle.

I wasn't a true believer back then, not in any meaningful way. I went to church on Sundays, I sat through the fellowship, but I had never felt that connection to a higher power that others talked about. It had always felt distant, abstract, something that other people experienced, but not me.

But now, standing in front of that gun cupboard, I couldn't deny the presence of something greater. It was as if the universe, or God, or whatever force was out there, had reached into my life and said,

"Not yet, mate."

I didn't know what to make of it, but I knew in my heart that this wasn't just some coincidence. It wasn't random. It was a message, one I wasn't prepared to fully comprehend, but undeniable at the same time. Such a moment may never happen to another person, but it happened to me.

I never told a sole and have carried that secret with me until now. To the outside world, everything went on as it always had. But inside, something had shifted. I didn't have the words for it then, but I know now that it was the beginning of something, a belief in a higher power, a recognition that I wasn't alone in the universe. It would become the foundation of my resilience, the quiet strength that would carry me through the darkest of times ahead.

Chapter 8

Cutting the First Wire

The neighbours saw what we had learned to hide. I remember vividly, because the mower kept clogging with damp clippings and my hands were shaking from the pull-start and the effort of pretending it was only the heat. A job undone is an insult you can see from the road, and the road mattered.

She stood at the front of the house and pointed at a strip I had missed, and even as she spoke I knew the script and could taste its last line: her voice rising, my throat tightening, the light going white around the edges like the world had narrowed to a keyhole. I won't write what followed except to say there was a sound that lives in my bones and then there were other sounds: the shock of a child's gasp on the other side of the hedge, the clatter of something dropped, a woman's voice sharp with a word that meant stop, then the kind of silence that notices itself.

After, the yard looked the same to anyone driving by: lawn so neat it could shame a parade, roses behaving, fruit trees pretending patience. The only difference was the way my skin remembered the air.

An hour later a car came up the drive, white, official, the kind of clean that makes you double-check your shoes. Two strangers stepped out in sensible clothing and kind faces they wore like uniforms. They spoke gently. They asked for tea. They asked for

"a quick chat, if you don't mind," in the tone of people trained to disarm a room with warmth.

She had met them with a tray already set, as if she had known they were coming and had decided what their visit would mean before they took their first breaths under our roof. Her laugh was elegant and light.

"Of course," she said, "come in," and then, to me,

"Mind your manners."

They sat in the room we weren't allowed to use, on the couch I had been told could bruise if you looked at it too harshly. They asked about school, about chores, about whether we felt safe at home, and the words sounded like birds that didn't know where to land. I tried on the answers I had learned in church and in kitchens and in hallways and picked the ones least likely to make the weather change.

She answered for us when she could, correcting a pronoun here, smoothing a pause there, adding a bright note of virtue where a shadow might have gathered.

"I run a tight ship," she said proudly, which in our house meant people were cargo.

"Standards are so important these days."

The woman nodded and wrote something that I tried not to see. The man asked Dad a soft question and he said,

"We do our best," a voice that made the room sag.

It was now clear to everyone in the room that some truths don't fit in forms.

They left with brochures about support and a promise to be in touch that sounded like a decision had already been made not to be. I watched the car drive away down the neat road and felt something move inside me that wasn't relief. If rescue could be charmed at the door, what did that make of hope? That night the house shrank by half. We ate carefully. We breathed carefully. After the dishes she called me to the hallway with the same tone she used for "Dinner" and "Smile." I won't write what happened then either, only that it cost more because other people had dared to imagine we might be worth saving. When I went to bed my body hummed like the mower had installed itself under my skin and wasn't going to stop.

After that, the neighbours' eyes learned the art of sliding. On the verge, at the letterbox, in the split second where a hello fits, their faces softened then hardened then turned. The little girl with the bike waved with a question in her fingers and her mother touched her wrist and the wave fell.

I started mowing before the sun had the chance to tell on us. The lines looked sharper in the early light; from the road you could almost hear them say everything is fine.

Kylie had recently returned from boarding school and had said very little for the first week, and then said too much in one sentence.

"Even rescue can be another kind of cage," she murmured, as we tied the new roses, thorns catching in our sleeves like insistence.

I nodded. It wasn't rage I felt, it was the grief that comes when you learn how systems love their forms more than your bruises. She handed me a little blue notebook and said,

"Write where no one can clean it."

So I began to keep a quiet ledger of weather and work and the ways a family can be a performance that wins applause from people who don't stay for the encore.

Dad spent more hours in the shed. He tuned the radio to the kind of cricket that lasts all day so the house would assume he was listening and leave him alone. Sometimes he set two bottles on the bench and said,

"Ten minutes," and we would drink the sugar like a secret, eyes on the open door, ears tuned for her steps.

We never spoke about the visit from the officials. He looked at my hands instead, the skinned knuckles, the green crescent of lawn under a nail, and said,

"Wear gloves."

It was as close to a blessing as we were going to get.

High school made me taller in ways no one could measure. The bus windows showed me other fences, other hedges, other houses trying to be the right sort of sky. Between periods I learned the geometry of exits and the mathematics of leaving without being seen. I kept my face pleasant and my feet ready. When teachers praised my neat work, I felt both proud and slightly ill. Neatness had always been the language of survival and now it was a grade.

Back home, the garden grew into a calendar of demands. Roses want winter more than spring if you ask them properly. Trees ask for shape the way a question asks for an answer you've already chosen. Lawns ask to be mown because they are show-offs. She kept score in clipped stems and the kind of compliments that begin with "I don't know how you manage" and end with "Standards these days."

Sometimes the retired man next door would lean over the fence and say,

"That's a lot of work for a kid," and she would appear with lemonade and the kind of smile that makes men feel they've misread something.

"He likes it," she'd say, and I would hold the glass and make my face a weather report that suggested fine.

There is a place at the back of that property where the manicured world gives up and the treeline begins, a seam stitched badly on purpose. I found it the first week and kept

91

returning as if the earth had left a door ajar just for me. The trees and the grass there are allowed to be themselves. The wire fence there vibrates the true note of boundary. From that spot you can see the town as a suggestion and the road as a decision and the sky as a dare. I went there whenever I could, even if it was only for the length of a breath and pressed my fingers into the soil until they looked like I belonged to something that couldn't be purchased. I didn't pray. I just listened. The land said what it had always said: keep breathing.

The day the "For Sale" sign from our past was replaced by a new sign that said some version of Home, she stood with her arms folded and surveyed the neat empire as if it might salute.

"A proper garden," she said, satisfied, and named the roses after virtues she never practiced.

When visitors came from town and said how grand, how tasteful, how very civilized, she said,

"We've moved up in the world," and no one asked from where.

Dad shook hands on the paved drive and tried not to look like a man averaging shame and pride. Kylie passed plates and saved her voice for pages no one else could read. I poured ginger ale and counted the beats between compliments and orders.

Chapter 9

Where the Hedge Ends

Years later, people who prefer happy endings would ask when things began to change for me, and I would think of this chapter of land with its obedient hedge and its hidden seam and say, "Here," even though nothing useful happened, because sometimes the beginning of leaving is only a direction you hold in your body like a compass you're not ready to trust.

The fence line taught me to measure the difference between ownership and boundary. One takes. The other keeps you from falling off the edge of yourself.

On the last evening of the first term at the new school, I finished mowing as the light thinned to a coin and stood at that seam again. Behind me, the house glowed with the kind of brightness that pretends to be welcome. Ahead, the yard carried a wind that did not ask where I had been. I could hear the little girl next door trying to whistle and her mother telling her to practice without spitting; I could hear Dad's radio counting overs; I could hear the roses insist they were more than show.

I put my hand on the wire, and the wire sang.

"One day," I said, and the words didn't feel like a wish anymore. They felt like a line drawn gently but firmly on a map only I would ever see.

Then I put the mower away exactly where it belonged, wiped the green from my hands, and went inside when she called, because sometimes the bravest thing you can do at fifteen is live long enough to know what you're walking toward.

By spring the place looked exactly as she had imagined. A green geometry of conformity. The hedges had found their shape, the roses obeyed, and even the air seemed ironed. Visitors said the property had "come alive," though it was only learning how to pose. Every weekend brought something to polish, a tap that spotted, a hinge that complained, a patch of lawn that grew faster than the rest. She kept a notebook of tasks as thick as a phone book. I learned that nothing finished, it only started again.

In the shed, Dad built things that didn't need building. Shelves for tools, boxes for nails, a bench that could hold a car if you believed hard enough. The radio was his clock; when the six o'clock news came on he'd turn the volume down so the world stayed small. Sometimes he let me sit on an upturned bucket and hand him screws. We didn't speak much, but silence there was different, less like a warning, more like permission. When I asked why he spent so much time in here he said,

"It's quiet," and the words landed heavier than he meant them to.

Neighbours stopped stopping by. The day the officials had come was the last day anyone knocked without invitation. The man with the lemons still waved from his car but didn't cross the fence again. The little girl's bike appeared at the edge of our drive only once more before her mother called her back. In the evenings, when she shouted goodnight from somewhere out of sight, I shouted it back even if no one was listening. That was the only part of me that reached beyond the hedge.

Kylie spent most of her time at boarding school or in her room. She'd found a friend whose parents lived on the other side of town and sometimes stayed there on weekends. They laugh a lot she told me once, almost guilty. The kind of laugh that doesn't check who's listening. When she was home, she helped in the kitchen, humming under her breath until the sound made Mum turn her head.

"Don't make that noise," Mum said.

Kylie smiled without opening her mouth and went on humming anyway, just softer. I think that was the bravest thing she ever did.

There were small mercies in the new routine. The school bus came early enough that I could leave before the house was fully awake. The fifteen-minute ride through town to school felt like borrowed time. Streets with shops, kids who shouted across the aisles, the smell of some girl's perfume that wasn't hers. In those minutes I almost belonged to ordinary life. Coming home was the reverse, each kilometre shedding laughter, shrinking into the shape expected of me. By the time I reached the gate I'd already rehearsed how to sound grateful.

Summer pressed down like a thumb. The mower coughed through the heat, the sky turned to tin, and every movement left a smear of salt on skin. She said sweat was common too, so I learned to dry my face before she saw it.

On the hottest afternoon the mower finally gave up, its exhaust coughing black smoke. I stood there, the machine silent at my feet, and for one glorious second the world stopped asking. Then her voice came from the laundry window:

"Well, don't just stand there. Find your father and fix it."

I wanted to tell her it was beyond fixing, that some things die because they're tired, not broken. Instead, I said,

"Yes," and went to the shed to find Dad.

He looked at the mower, then at me.

"You don't have to rush," he said quietly.

I waited for the rest, the warning, the lecture, but it didn't come. He passed me a cold bottle and said,

"Sit a minute."

The radio hummed. Outside, the insects were loud enough to be a wall of sound. For the first time in a long time, I let my body stop pretending it wasn't exhausted. He said,

"You'll be taller than me soon."

"Maybe," I said.

It was nothing and everything. When I stood to go, he added,

"Sometimes it's all right to rest. Just don't let her see."

That was the closest he ever came to rebellion.

At night the house clicked and sighed, settling into its new shape. Through the open window I could hear the distant hum of other lives, cars on the highway, a dog barking, the faint echo of music from somewhere that wasn't ours. I began to keep a notebook like Kylie's, writing in tiny letters so the words could hide between the lines: what the sky looked like before dawn, how the air changed before anger, how silence could be both shield and cell. I didn't know it yet, but those notes were the first pieces of another self assembling quietly beneath the one she had built.

By the end of the second year, the garden had learned its script and so had I. When people asked how we liked the move, I said it was wonderful. When they praised the lawn, I said thank you. When they said how lucky we were, I agreed. Luck, I had discovered, is just what other people call survival when they don't have to live it.

The fence line still marked the edge of everything, humming softly at night like a low note only I could hear. I would walk there after dark, barefoot on cool grass, the house a glow behind me, the town a faint shimmer ahead. The wire carried the wind's voice and, if you listened long enough, it almost sounded like promise.

Part II — The Breaking Point

Chapter 10

Moving Away and Losing Myself

Leaving didn't look heroic; it looked like packing a single suitcase in a room that had never really belonged to me. The night before I left for university, the house hummed its usual disapproval, kettle boiling too long, clock ticking too loudly, her footsteps measuring control one last time. She didn't talk about pride or possibility, just cost.

"We've spent enough," she said.

"Make it worth it."

I wanted to tell her that worth was the thing I was going to look for, but some truths are safer unsaid. Dad loaded the car in silence, the air thick with things we'd both decided not to feel.

The drive to the city was four hours of half-sentences. He pointed out landmarks, told stories about fences he'd mended, neighbours who'd moved away, weather that refused to cooperate. Each one was a translation of what he couldn't say outright: I'll miss you. Be careful. Don't forget who you are. When we reached the university gates, he gripped the steering wheel like it might hold him steady.

"You'll do all right," he said finally.

I nodded. He didn't get out. I watched the car until it was just another piece of light swallowed by traffic, and only then did I breathe.

The dormitory smelled of paint and possibility. The first night I couldn't sleep because no one shouted. The quiet was too wide, the freedom too loud. For days I walked the campus as if waiting for someone to tell me where to stand. I learned to introduce myself without flinching, to laugh without asking permission.

People said university was about discovery; they didn't warn you that discovering yourself can feel like walking on a floor that isn't finished yet.

That's when I met her, the woman who would teach me that you can run from a place but still carry its weather. She was older by a year, confident in the way people are when they've never had to make themselves small. In a lecture on developmental psychology, she argued with the professor and won, and I fell into her orbit like a moth that thought fire was light.

Her name, let's call her Anna, was a song I didn't know but wanted to whistle. She spoke fast, laughed faster, and looked at me like I was both puzzle and mirror. I mistook the attention for love. Maybe it was, in its own damaged dialect.

Anna had that same mix of certainty and volatility I recognised from home. She could make you feel chosen one minute and invisible the next. When she smiled, the room leaned toward her; when she turned away, it felt like exile. She didn't know she reminded me of my mother, and I didn't know I was looking for a familiar kind of storm. Freud would have called it repetition compulsion. I just called it gravity.

Our relationship moved quickly, as if we were both afraid to pause. She liked that I listened; I liked that she talked. We built a small world out of late-night coffee, borrowed cigarettes, and the illusion that understanding was enough to fix what history had broken. When she grew sharp, I grew quieter; when she apologised, I learned to smile as if forgiveness were the same as safety. It was a dance I already knew, only now the music was different.

I studied hard, psychology, literature, any subject that promised answers to why people hurt the ones who love them. My professors praised my insight.

"You see what others miss," one said.

I wanted to tell him that missing things was a luxury. Seeing everything was survival. But I took the compliment and filed it with the rest of my disguises. At night I wrote essays that sounded objective and journals that weren't. The words began to split into two languages: one for marks, one for mercy.

On break I went home. The house had changed again, new furniture, new curtains, new rules. My younger brothers were taller, louder, untouchable.

Kylie had moved out by then, found work in another town.

"She's made her bed," Mum said, meaning she'd chosen freedom over duty.

Dad looked smaller, or maybe I was just seeing him clearly for the first time. He asked about my studies, nodded at the right times, and when I told him about Anna his eyes flickered like someone hearing bad weather coming.

"Just be careful," he said.

"Not everyone who looks like home, is."

I didn't understand until much later how much wisdom can hide inside a single warning.

During that visit the air between Mum and me grew thick again. She found fault in my clothes, my posture, my ideas.

"You think too much," she said, as if thought were a stain that needed scrubbing.

One night, after too many words about nothing, she said,

"Don't forget who made you what you are."

I wanted to answer, you did, but my voice stayed in my throat. Later, alone in the shed, I opened Dad's old gun cupboard. The smell of gunpowder and metal hit me like a memory that hadn't aged. I didn't pick anything up; I just looked. The thought that passed through me wasn't about ending, it was about quiet, about finally making the noise stop. Then I closed the door, locked it, and sat on the cold floor until the feeling changed shape.

When I returned to university, I threw myself into study. Anna called it obsession. I called it control. I was chasing a version of peace I'd seen only in other people's eyes. The further I ran toward knowledge, the more I realised I was studying my own reflection through a microscope. Trauma, attachment, conditioning, they weren't theories; they were my family tree.

By the time the year ended, Anna and I were already fading. She needed chaos to feel alive; I needed order to survive. We mistook need for love until it broke under its own weight. The night she left, she said,

"You're so calm it's like talking to a wall."

I wanted to tell her the wall was the only part of me that ever kept anyone safe. Instead I said,

"I'm sorry," and meant it for everything.

I didn't go home that summer. I found a room near the river, worked in a bookshop that smelled of dust and coffee, and learned the pleasure of being nobody. For the first time I could choose silence without fear.

Sometimes, walking along the water, I'd hear the wind catch on the bridge and hum a note that sounded almost like the fence line. It didn't hurt anymore. It just reminded me that survival isn't a story you finish; it's one you learn to carry.

I didn't know it yet, but the real reckoning wasn't waiting in a classroom or a lover's arms - it was waiting inside me, biding its time like weather on the horizon. The past has a way of finding you even when you change the scenery; it travels light, no luggage, just memory and reflex.

The more I learned about the mind, the more I recognised my own fingerprints on the glass. Every pattern had a name now - projection, trauma bond, complex PTSD - but names didn't make them disappear. They only gave shape to what I'd been carrying all along.

When the semester ended, the city of Newcastle felt too loud, the river too wide. I told myself I needed a break, a few weeks at home to reset, to make peace with what I'd left behind. What I really wanted was proof that leaving had meant something - that I could return and not be that boy anymore.

But the house didn't care about who I'd become; it remembered who I was. The rooms still held the same air, thick and watchful. The whip still hung by the kitchen door, older now but patient. Even the light seemed filtered through her eyes.

That was the summer the noise inside me reached a pitch I couldn't outrun. It started as a whisper, then a drone, then a call - the kind that doesn't ask for answers, only endings. The line was thin that day and I stood firmly on it.

Chapter 11

The Light That Stayed

Mornings came softer after that, as if the world had heard and decided to tread more carefully. The sky didn't change, the chores didn't stop, the house didn't loosen its grip, but somewhere inside me, something small had refused to die. I didn't call it faith. That felt too big, too polished, a word that belonged to pulpits and people who never had to look down the barrel of their own silence. What I had was quieter. It lived under the ribs, a pulse that said keep breathing.

The days blurred in the way ordinary survival does. University, work, garden, sleep. The drought deepened and the land cracked and waited. Every morning, I watched the horizon for a hint of rain and wondered if belief worked the same way, if you waited long enough, would something finally break open? I didn't ask God for anything specific; I just asked not to vanish. That seemed small enough to grant.

Sometimes, when Dad and I worked side by side, cutting or fixing or hauling, he'd sing under his breath, an old country tune without words. I used to think he was just filling the silence. Later, I realised it was prayer in disguise, the kind men who don't talk much still manage to say. Never mentioned that night in the mancave; he didn't know. But there were moments when he looked at me and I wondered if somewhere in him he felt the shift too, a tremor in the air that said something held.

Mum went on performing perfection for the neighbours. The garden was her gospel now, every bloom a verse about control, every clipped hedge a sermon on appearances. She'd say, "God helps those who help themselves," as if it explained everything. I'd nod, thinking that maybe He also helps the ones who almost don't.

Kylie's letters came sporadically, ink smudged by hurry or tears, I could never tell which. She wrote about freedom like it was a foreign country she was still learning the language of.

"You'd like it here," she said once.

"People ask how you are and mean it."

I kept her letters folded in the back of a book I read them over and over until the spine broke, proof that connection could travel distance without asking permission.

The months that followed stretched long but not empty. I began to notice small mercies hiding in the routine. The smell of rain before it arrived, the moment just before dawn when the magpies tuned their throats, the way my brothers' laughter sometimes reminded me that innocence hadn't entirely left the building. They were still "blood," still favoured, but they were also just boys. It took me years to learn that resentment and compassion can live in the same house.

Faith grew slowly, like something that doesn't want to startle you. I found it in unexpected places, in the steady rhythm of the mower, in the weight of a book, in the single breath between one heartbeat and the next. It wasn't about churches or hymns or polished shoes; it was about survival being seen and named as grace. I started to believe that maybe staying had a purpose.

The world outside our fence began to pull harder. Friends talked about the future like it was a road waiting for them; I still thought of it as a gate I'd have to learn how to open. I didn't have plans, not really. Just a promise I'd made to something larger than myself that night in the mancave, that if I got to keep living, I'd make the life count for something. I didn't know what that meant yet, but meaning, I was discovering, doesn't arrive as a map. It grows from the ground you've been buried in.

When graduation came, the town turned out to smile for photographs. Parents shook hands, siblings cheered, the air smelled of hairspray and hope. Mum stood beside me for the picture, her hand light on my shoulder, her smile trained for the camera.

"You've made us proud," she said, and for once I didn't flinch.

I let her have that version of the story. Pride can be a kind of peace too.

That night I walked to the edge of the property, where the manicured lawn met the stubborn field, and stood by the fence line that had raised me. The stars were the same ones that had watched everything, indifferent but loyal. I thought about the boy I'd been, the one who believed leaving was the only way to survive, and I wanted to tell him that staying had its own kind of victory. You can walk through hell and still come out carrying light.

I didn't have a plan, only a direction. Forward. Whatever waited there, I'd meet it with the faith I hadn't asked for but had been given anyway. The faith that arrived in the sound of an empty gun and the whisper that followed: Not yet, mate. That voice, that mercy, that impossible grace, it hadn't left. It was the light that stayed.

Chapter 12

Becoming the Man I Was Told to Be

Leaving home wasn't a single day, it was a series of small departures that no one noticed. First the job applications, then the interviews, then the promise of a paycheck that could buy a kind of freedom. By the time the moving boxes appeared, the house had already stopped being mine. She didn't hug me goodbye; she smoothed my collar and said,

"Make us proud."

Dad shook my hand like we were business partners. The drive away felt less like escape

119

and more like exhaling after years of holding my breath.

My first job was at a school just far enough from home to feel like another world but close enough that the weather still smelled familiar. The classrooms buzzed with noise I didn't have to fear. Children laughed without checking who was listening. The first time a student called me sir, I turned to see who they meant. It took months to believe they meant me.

Teaching became a mirror and every child a reflection of the person I might have been if kindness had come sooner. I told myself I was there to give them what I never had, patience, safety, the permission to be imperfect. Maybe I was teaching myself, too.

The staffroom was its own ecosystem, coffee, gossip, exhaustion, hope. I learned quickly that schools are families with better lighting. There were hierarchies, favourites, secrets passed between cups of coffee. I stayed mostly on the edges, watching, learning the politics of belonging. One afternoon a colleague said,

"You're quiet, but you notice everything."

I smiled. Observation had been my only real education.

Outside work, life felt like a blank page. I filled it with long walks, second hand books, and the illusion that distance could erase inheritance. But habits are loyal creatures. I still sought approval, still mistook control for love, still said yes when I meant maybe. The fence line was gone, but I carried its echo inside me. Boundaries were still something other people had.

Then there was her, the woman who would become my first wife. I'll call her Claire. She was warmth and fire and a challenge I couldn't name. The first time we met, she laughed at something I said and touched my arm lightly, and my body lit up like a signal flare. It wasn't just attraction, it was recognition. I didn't know then that familiarity and safety can feel the same at first. She came from a world full of noise, ambition, and sharp corners. I mistook that for strength. She mistook my quiet for peace. We were both wrong.

In those early years I worked hard, built a reputation, ticked the boxes that make a life look stable. Marriage, mortgage, and respectability. People said I was lucky, and I nodded. But luck, I knew, was just endurance rebranded. The routines of adulthood were easier to survive than childhood, but they carried the same rhythm, pleasing, performing, pretending. Faith flickered but never went out; it lived somewhere between the hours, in the spaces I still couldn't fill with noise.

At night, when the house was dark and the quiet vibration of the refrigerator was the only sound, I'd think about that boy on the fence line, the one who whispered one day. I realised he'd been right, but he hadn't told me that freedom comes with its own set of chains, the ones you forge out of memory, love, and the longing to belong.

The first months of teaching felt like living in borrowed light. Every lesson was a performance, chalk dust on my hands, eyes on the clock, the quiet scream of thirty stories intersecting. I loved it, even the chaos. When a student's face lit with understanding it was like a match struck in a dark field. I learned that praise, given honestly, could change the shape of a day. I also learned that some children came to school hungry, frightened, exhausted. I recognised the look, it was the same one that used to stare back at me from bathroom mirrors. I promised myself they would never feel unseen.

After class I stayed behind, tidying, rewriting, building order out of the mess. The Principal called it dedication. I knew it was control. Routine was still the only language I trusted. If I planned every hour, the past couldn't ambush me.

Then there was Claire. She arrived one winter morning to cover another teacher's class, hair pulled back, eyes sharp and a very short summer dress. She spoke fast, moved faster, filled rooms the way storms fill skies. Within weeks we were sharing coffee, stories, silences. She asked about my family, so I gave her the edited version, hard-working parents, country upbringing, nothing remarkable. She smiled like she didn't quite believe me but didn't push.

"You've got depth," she said.

"Like someone who's read the end of the book before the beginning."

I didn't tell her I'd lived the ending and was still trying to rewrite it.

We married too quickly, as people often do when they think love will finish the work therapy never started. The day felt like sunlight after years of drizzle. Everyone said we looked happy, and for a while we were. She loved the way I listened, I loved the way she spoke as if certainty were a virtue. But somewhere between vows and bills, the old rhythm returned, the need to earn affection, the quiet apology for existing. She didn't mean to take advantage of it. I didn't know how to stop offering it. We were both repeating what we'd been taught, that love is maintenance, not mystery.

Teaching became my refuge again. I took extra duties, late meetings, weekend sports supervision, anything that kept me busy enough to call exhaustion devotion. Claire called it ambition. I called it staying alive. The staffroom talk turned from holidays to mortgages, from books to babies. I nodded in all the right places, but inside I felt the distance growing, a hollow that no amount of success could fill.

Faith changed too. It was less about asking and more about listening. Sometimes, walking home after late marking sessions, I'd pass the small stone church at the edge of town. The door was often unlocked. I'd sit in the back pew, not praying exactly, just breathing in the quiet. The air there felt honest, old timber, candle wax, dust. I didn't ask for guidance, I asked for understanding. The answer when it came was simple. Keep going.

Years passed like that, small victories, silent retreats, the steady construction of a life that looked right from a distance. Then one evening at a staff conference I met another teacher who spoke about her students the way people speak about their own children. She said,

"Every kid deserves at least one adult who won't walk away."

The sentence stayed with me. I realised I had become that adult without noticing. The boy who once believed no one would stay had become the man who refused to leave. It wasn't redemption exactly, but it was purpose, and purpose, I'd learned, can save you as completely as faith.

Still, under the surface, the old stories waited. You can't grow up in a house of performance and not become an actor. I wore competence like a costume. Even love became a script I followed too carefully. Claire began to notice the distance.

"You're here but not," she said once.

I wanted to tell her that's what survival looks like, that being present can still feel like hiding, but all I managed was,

"I'm tired."

She nodded, and the space between us solidified into habit.

What I didn't know was that life was already writing its next chapter: new cities, new faces, the tangled intersection between respectability and the world that hides beneath it. That story would take me far from the classroom and deep into the kind of truth polite people never discuss over dinner. But that as they say, is another book.

Chapter 13

The Company We Keep

The town looked harmless from the outside, rows of jacarandas, an Italian bakery that smelled of sugar and spice, parents who nodded to me in the local supermarket as if trust were part of the groceries. But every place has its undertow, and I was learning that respectability often floats on top of something restless.

Claire and I had moved into a small brick house near the school. She filled it with colour, laughter, friends who spoke too loudly at dinner. I filled it with silence and lesson plans. On weekends we hosted barbecues where everyone talked about mortgages and rising prices and the way the city crept closer each year. I laughed when I was supposed to, flipped steaks, refilled glasses. From the fence you would have sworn we were happy.

One evening a colleague brought a new face, a man she introduced simply as Mark. He was charming in the way people are when they've made a habit of it. Crisp shirt, easy grin, stories that walked the edge between believable and not. He spoke about opportunity the way some speak about faith.

"Connections," he said, "are what make the world work."

Everyone nodded, even those who didn't understand the machinery behind the word. When he left, Claire said,

"He knows people." I didn't ask what kind.

In the months that followed, Mark reappeared, at fundraisers, at the pub after school events, at dinners Claire organised to feel important. He always seemed to bring someone new, always a degree removed from the kind of respectability I was trying to maintain. They spoke about business ventures, logistics, import and export, words that sounded legitimate until you listened too long. I wasn't naïve; I'd seen enough shadows to recognise one when it passed over me. But part of me, the part still hungry for belonging, stayed close anyway. The company you keep, I was learning, is sometimes the one that promises you a version of yourself you want to believe in.

Work at school remained steady. I rose through the ranks, took on leadership roles, became the reliable one. But outside those walls another version of me was growing, one that laughed too easily, that enjoyed the pull of risk. Claire thrived in that world. She liked the attention, the talk of influence. I watched her sparkle across tables and felt both pride and unease. She would say,

"You need to loosen up," and I would smile, thinking of how many times I'd heard that phrase in another lifetime, from another woman whose storms I once mistook for warmth.

The first time I met Mark's circle outside of a social event, it was by accident, or maybe inevitability. A favour for a friend of a friend: a ride, a conversation, a promise to introduce someone to a contact. Nothing illegal, nothing dramatic, just proximity. But proximity has gravity. Before long I was attending gatherings that stretched late into the night, conversations about politics and profit weaving with whispers about people who made things disappear, debts, reputations, evidence. It felt like standing on a familiar edge, only this time the danger came with linen napkins and expensive wine.

I told myself it was networking, harmless. But at night, lying awake beside Claire, I could feel the past humming under my ribs again, the old instinct that told me when charm hides control, when generosity is a leash. I thought I'd left that behind with the fence line, but it had only changed its uniform.

Faith remained, though smaller now, quieter. I still visited the church sometimes, still sat in the back pew, still waited for the kind of silence that answers. One night after another of those dinners, I found myself there again. The candles had burned down to their last inch, wax pooled like small confessions. I asked, not for guidance, but for recognition. The answer came the way it always did. Not in words but in the sudden, steady calm that said, you know this pattern. You've survived it before.

I went home and stood in the dark kitchen listening to the distant sound of tyres on the highway. The world I'd built was beginning to shift again, edges blurring between right and almost-right. I didn't yet know that this was the threshold to a story big enough for another book, one that would carry my name into rooms I never meant to enter. I only knew that the company you keep can either heal or haunt you, and sometimes you don't know which until the door closes behind you.

The cracks always start small. You don't hear them at first; they sound like everyday life, missed dinners, laughter that doesn't include you, a glance that lingers half a second too long. Claire had grown restless. She called it ambition, said she wanted to move up, to be seen, to matter. I understood that hunger; it was the same one that had driven me once. But hers began to pull her somewhere I couldn't follow.

There was a man at her work, another teacher, sharp suit, sharper smile. I met him once at a staff function. He talked too much and looked at her like he already knew the answer to a question he hadn't asked yet. She said he was just a friend, that they were planning a curriculum project together. I nodded because disbelief felt like a betrayal worse than the truth. You learn, growing up in a house of control, to ignore what you can't fix.

For months I convinced myself that nothing was wrong. We still went to dinners, still smiled for photos, still played the part. But at night she turned away in bed, and I recognised the shape of absence. When I asked if she was happy, she said,

"You're overthinking again," the same phrase my mother used to quiet questions she didn't want to answer.

I didn't ask again.

The day the truth arrived began like any other, marking papers, phone vibrating on the desk, a number I didn't recognise. When I answered, a woman's voice came through, low and shaking.

"You don't know me," she said, "but I think you need to come."

She named an address, her tone halfway between fury and heartbreak.

"Your wife's here," she added. "And so's my husband." Then the line went dead.

I drove without memory of the road, the kind of drive where every second folds into the next. When I arrived, the street was already busy, curtains twitching, the sharp smell of rain on concrete. The front door was open. Inside, chaos had the shape of truth. The man was on the floor, bleeding from a split lip, shirt torn. The woman, his wife, stood over him, chest heaving, a force of nature reclaiming her sky. Claire was against the wall, crying, whispering apologies that didn't seem meant for anyone in particular. No one noticed me at first. I didn't speak. I just stood there, watching a life I thought I knew collapse into something I no longer recognised.

When his wife finally saw me, she froze.

"You should know," she said, voice cracking into anger.

"They've been at it for months."

There was no malice, just exhaustion. She looked at me like someone offering proof they never wanted to give. I nodded, because what else was there to do? Claire tried to follow as I left, calling my name, but the sound felt foreign. I got into the car, turned the key, and drove until the sky changed colour.

People say heartbreak feels like pain, but it doesn't. It feels like absence, like every sound has been muted except your own breathing. That night I sat on the edge of the bed staring at the empty half of the mattress and realised I wasn't surprised. Betrayal doesn't shock those who've lived inside it before. It just changes faces.

In the weeks that followed, the story spread the way stories do in small towns, half-truths stitched with speculation. Claire moved out, stayed with friends, said she needed space. I let her have it.

The silence that followed wasn't peaceful, but it was honest. For the first time in years, I wasn't pretending. The house felt lighter without the weight of performance, though I hated the reason for it.

The divorce was quiet, procedural, the kind of ending that leaves no witnesses. She cried at the signing; I didn't. There's a point where grief becomes maintenance, just another task to get through. When she left the room, she said,

"You'll find someone else."

I didn't answer.

Afterwards, I walked to the church again. The candles were still burning, their small flames steady and unbothered. I didn't ask for forgiveness, I asked for clarity. The answer was silence, but this time it felt like understanding. Sometimes endings are mercy in disguise.

I threw myself into work again, taught until my voice went hoarse, coached sports, mentored new teachers. From the outside, it looked like resilience. Inside, it felt like rebuilding a house on the same cracked foundation. But there was one difference now, I knew the cracks were there. And knowing is the beginning of change.

Part III — Breaking the Mirror

Chapter 14

Cracks Quietly Appear

There was no single day I decided to forgive her. It happened the way dawn does, slowly, almost unnoticed, until you realise the dark has lifted. The years after the divorce blurred into work, recovery, and the quiet art of staying upright. Faith changed shape again. It stopped asking for miracles and started whispering questions: What now? Who are you without your wounds?

When I was forty, I saw her reflection before I saw her, the faint silhouette of my mother in a shop window, older, smaller, but unmistakably her. She hadn't changed much; the world still bent itself to her idea of how things should look.

"You've filled out," she said instead of hello.

I smiled because it was easier than answering. We talked about safe things, the weather, the garden, who'd married whom. But beneath it, a current moved, decades of words unsaid.

She wanted to know if I had met my biological mother. I told her no, and that I didn't intend to. The answer seemed to bother her more than I expected.

"Don't you want to know where you come from?" she asked.

I wanted to say, I already do, half of it is standing in front of me. But I didn't. I'd learned that some truths only create more noise. Instead, I said,

"I'm where I need to be."

It was the first time I'd seen confusion in her eyes. Control doesn't know what to do with acceptance.

After that meeting, she began her own search. I don't know if it was guilt or curiosity, but she wrote letters, made calls, asked questions I had already stopped needing answers to. For years she'd wanted to shape my story, now she wanted to rewrite its beginning. I let her. Maybe she needed to believe that finding the woman who gave me life would somehow make her the woman who saved it.

Meanwhile, my own healing work deepened. Therapy, journals, long nights of unlearning. I began to read about narcissism, not the cartoon version, but the clinical, complex kind that hides behind charm and structure. Every paragraph was a mirror, every symptom a ghost I recognised. But somewhere in the reading, the anger softened. I started to see her not as a monster, but as a blueprint of unhealed pain. It didn't excuse what she'd done but it explained why she'd never known another way to be.

Forgiveness didn't arrive as a single act. It was a practice. A discipline. Some days it felt like grace, other days like surrender. I forgave because carrying the weight any longer felt like agreeing with it.

When I finally spoke the words out loud, to no-one but the night, it felt less like letting her off the hook and more like letting myself out of a cage.

It started with small changes - the kind that don't announce themselves until you look back and realise how far the ground has shifted. She forgot birthdays, repeated stories, lost track of names. At first, I thought it was performance again, another act to keep attention tethered. But then I saw it wasn't control, this time it was confusion. The sharpness that once cut everyone around her had dulled into something almost fragile. It was disorienting to see the woman who ruled through precision now fumbling for words. Part of me pitied her. Part of me wanted to believe this was penance.

She called often during those years. Always the same opening:

"Have you found her yet?" meaning my biological mother.

My answer never changed, though the tone softened over time.

"No, Mum. I'm not looking."

The pause that followed was heavy with things she'd never say out loud - regret, resentment, maybe even love, though she would never use the word. She'd sigh, adjust her voice back to its formal setting, and ask about the weather. In her world, emotion was still something to be filed under appearances.

Her obsession with finding my biological mother became her last great project. She gathered information like prayer beads - dates, hospital names, adoption agencies, fragments of old letters. She believed that finding this woman would complete her, not me.

"Don't you want closure?" she asked once.

"You're the one who needs it," I said quietly.

She didn't answer, and I didn't expect her to. People like her never stop looking for control, they just rename it care.

It was around then that I began to change the language I used for her. For decades I had called her a narcissist - privately, clinically, with the certainty that the label gave me power. But therapy has a way of replacing labels with mirrors. One day, after another session that left me hollow and tender, I caught myself thinking of her not as a villain but as a system glitch - someone wired differently, incapable of reading emotional code the way most people do. The word Asperger's appeared in my mind like a small mercy. Not as an excuse, but as an explanation.

I now call it the "Sheldon Cooper Effect" - a shorthand for understanding her logic, her rigidity, her black-and-white world. It didn't erase the past, but it changed the way I carried it. If she was broken circuitry, then maybe all her cruelty had been misfired intention, not malice. Maybe she wasn't punishing me - maybe she was trying to keep the world in a shape she could understand. That thought didn't absolve her, but it made forgiveness possible.

When I visited her after Dad passed, she was smaller than I remembered, the house quieter. The walls were still covered in framed perfection - family photos arranged like proof of success, everything in symmetry.

But the woman inside was fading around the edges.

"You've done well for yourself," she said, scanning me the way she used to inspect furniture polish.

"I've tried," I answered.

She smiled, a brittle attempt at warmth, and said,

"You always were a hard worker." It was the closest she had ever come to pride.

Before I left that day, she handed me an old envelope - yellowed, soft with years.

"If you ever change your mind," she said, "everything's in here."

I took it, not to open, but to end the conversation. She seemed relieved, as if handing over those papers had lightened something inside her. I didn't look at the contents until years later, and when I did, I realised she had done what I asked her not to.

The last time I saw her, she was in a care home, window seat facing the garden. Her eyes followed the light like a plant's, searching for something steady. She didn't recognise me at first. Then she did, and her voice softened.

"You've always been a good boy," she said, and for the first time in my life, I believed she meant it.

I told her I loved her. Not because she'd earned it, but because I finally understood love wasn't a transaction. It was a release.

Driving home that day, I thought about the fence line again - the invisible border that had once defined my world. I realised that forgiveness is just another kind of fence: it doesn't erase what's beyond it; it simply lets you decide which side you want to live on. For years, I'd built my life on survival. Now I wanted to build it on peace.

Chapter 15

The Sheldon Cooper Effect

Healing is rarely dramatic. It's paperwork, patterns, slow recognition. Years after that last visit to her, I began the real work, the kind that doesn't come with applause or even witnesses. I sat in rooms with white walls and kind-eyed therapists who asked me to tell the story again, only slower this time, so the body could keep up with the words. At first, I thought therapy was about understanding her. It took months to realise it was about understanding me.

I brought my history like an assignment: dates, events, cause and effect. The therapist smiled gently and said,

"Let's start with how it felt."

That question changed everything. I learned that emotion, for people raised in control, feels like danger until it becomes language. I learned that silence, once a shield, can become a cage. Week by week, I began to name things I had only ever survived.

Somewhere in those sessions the phrase the Sheldon Cooper Effect slipped out. I was trying to explain her precision, her bluntness, the way empathy seemed to confuse her.

"Like that character from the sitcom," I said, half-embarrassed.

"Brilliant, literal, but tone-deaf to feeling."

The therapist nodded.

"So, when you see her through that lens, what happens to your anger?"

I thought for a long time before answering. "It becomes sadness," I said.

"And then it becomes space."

That space was everything. It let me separate what she did from who I am. I stopped describing my childhood as damage and started describing it as data, a map of how people behave when love and fear speak the same language. Understanding didn't erase the pain, but it gave it context, and context is mercy.

I began to read obsessively again, psychology, trauma theory, memoirs of survival. Words that had once been escape became instruments of repair. I learned about narcissistic abuse, about the cycles of idealisation and devaluation, about the way children of control often become adults who apologise for breathing. Each page was a mirror I could investigate without flinching. I underlined sentences until the margins were crowded with my own voice saying, yes, this too.

Slowly, compassion replaced curiosity. I saw her spectrum not as cruelty alone but as confusion, her need for order, her terror of unpredictability, her endless pursuit of perfection as armour against chaos. If she was indeed neurodivergent, then her world had always been louder, brighter, more frightening than mine. Control had been her survival strategy, just as appeasement had been mine. We were two sides of the same fear, both trying to quiet the noise.

Forgiveness stopped being an act of virtue and became a form of hygiene. I cleaned the story until it could breathe. I talked to my children about boundaries, empathy, and repair. I made sure they knew that love isn't measured by obedience but by presence. Each conversation felt like rewiring the family line, replacing scarcity with grace.

There were setbacks, panic that arrived uninvited, old reflexes that whispered I wasn't enough, but now I recognised them as echoes, not instructions. The work of healing, I discovered, is not about erasing your ghosts; it's about teaching them new manners.

And then came the silence.

After years of analysing and explaining, I stopped speaking. I stopped trying to solve myself. In the quiet that followed, something ancient stirred, the subconscious mind, patient and persistent, stepping forward like a friend who had waited decades to be heard. I began to understand that silence isn't emptiness; it's communication in its purest form. Beneath the noise of survival, the mind whispers truths it can't shout.

At first, it felt like drifting, but soon the quiet became a current. Images surfaced, memories I hadn't seen in years, faces softened by compassion, scenes replayed not for pain but for perspective. It was as if the silence had unlocked a library I didn't know existed. This, I realised, was the mind healing itself.

And then came the revelation, shadow work. The part of therapy that no one warns you about, the confrontation with your own hidden self. The anger, the jealousy, the shame, the fear you pretend doesn't exist. I met them all in that silence. They weren't monsters. They were fragments of me, still waiting to be understood. The shadow, I learned, isn't the opposite of light, it's what gives light its meaning.

When I sat with those shadows, I realised that healing isn't about becoming better, it's about becoming whole. Every denied emotion, every suppressed truth was simply trying to come home. The work was in welcoming them back without judgment. Shadow work taught me that forgiveness is impossible without self-acceptance, and that peace begins where denial ends.

So I began to make silence a practice, not a pause. Each morning, before the world intruded, I sat with my breath and listened. Sometimes it brought memories; sometimes only calm. But always, it brought honesty. Silence was no longer absence, it was activation. The subconscious began to weave together everything therapy had pulled apart. I learned that the mind, when given space, doesn't destroy itself; it repairs. It connects dots you didn't even know existed. It shows you that your pain was never proof of weakness, it was evidence of endurance.

Now, when people ask me how I healed, I tell them the truth. I didn't. I listened. And the silence did the rest.

That practice, the marriage of quiet, shadow, and compassion, became the blueprint for my next life. It became the foundation of another book waiting to be written. A book about how silence activates the subconscious, how shadow work reveals the soul, and how both together lead you toward the only freedom that matters, living a life worth living.

The Light That Stayed

It's strange how a life can look linear on paper and yet feel like a spiral when you live it. I used to think healing meant getting as far away from the beginning as possible. Now I know it means walking back there with gentler eyes. Every path, every chapter, every silence was leading me here, to this quiet understanding that nothing was wasted - not even the suffering.

The fence line still exists somewhere in memory, stretching across dry paddocks, wire humming in the wind. When I picture it now, I see a boy standing there barefoot, waiting for permission to breathe. I want to tell him he made it. That he'll carry scars but also songs. That one day the word bought will stop meaning ownership and start meaning survival - that the transaction was never about money but about endurance exchanged for grace. That he was never property. He was a promise.

The mancave still smells of gunpowder, oil, and dust in my mind. I used to think that night was about death - about what almost happened. Now I understand it was about awakening. The empty rifle, the missing bullets, the click that saved me - all of it was silence intervening. The universe paused long enough to whisper not yet. That pause became a lifetime.

For years I ran from silence, afraid of what it might say. I filled every space with work, noise, people, purpose. But silence waited patiently, knowing I'd return. When I finally did, it welcomed me like an old teacher - no judgment, just presence. And in that stillness, everything began to make sense: faith, forgiveness, even pain. They were never enemies. They were languages of the same truth - that love is not the absence of suffering, but the courage to listen through it.

I sometimes wonder what my adoptive mother would think if she saw me now, sitting in the same quiet she once feared. Maybe she'd understand that order isn't control; it's harmony. Maybe she'd see that her attempt to create perfection only birthed persistence. Maybe she'd even smile. I hope so. In the end, she taught me the most valuable lesson of all: that people don't have to change for us to find peace - we just have to change the way we see them.

And then, after all those years of wondering, I found her - my biological mother. Not through anger or longing, but through a quiet curiosity that had ripened into readiness. Meeting her was like opening a window in a room I hadn't realised was still closed. Her warmth, her laughter, the softness in her voice - all of it felt like sunlight on skin I'd kept covered for too long. She was everything my adoptive mother wasn't: gentle where the other was sharp, accepting where the other was proud, unguarded where the other was afraid.

There was no bitterness in her story, only ache and love interwoven. She told me about the day she let me go, how the world gave her no choice and how she carried my name in her thoughts even when the years blurred. Listening to her, I understood something new: that love denied its expression doesn't die - it waits. And when it's finally allowed to speak, it doesn't accuse; it forgives.

Finding her didn't erase the past; it reframed it. It gave the story balance - nature beside nurture, compassion beside control. Where one woman taught me endurance, the other taught me grace. Between them, I finally saw myself whole.

The faith that began as desperation has become direction. I don't pray for rescue anymore. I pray for awareness - for the courage to keep meeting the parts of myself that still flinch, still ache, still long to be seen. Because the truth is, healing isn't a destination; it's a relationship - with yourself, with silence, and with whatever higher power holds you when words fail.

Every morning now, before the world wakes, I sit in stillness. I breathe. I listen. Sometimes I hear nothing. Sometimes I hear everything - the wind through gum trees, the faint echo of magpies, the heartbeat that almost wasn't. And now, sometimes, I hear her voice too - the one that gave me life, not just survival.

And in that soundless moment, I realise that all I ever needed was already here:

The love that waited,

the forgiveness that grew,

the light that stayed.

Author's Note

When I began writing We Bought YOU, I didn't know I was writing a book. I thought I was trying to remember. What I learned instead is that memory is not a record, it's a mirror. Every story you revisit shows you a version of yourself you hadn't yet met. This book is that meeting.

To those who have walked through silence, who have lived behind fences, real or invisible, this story is for you. You are not alone. You were never broken; you were adapting. Surviving. Listening. The world may have taught you to hide your wounds, but healing begins when you look at them with tenderness, not shame.

Writing this story was a form of shadow work, the process of meeting the parts of myself I had avoided for decades. In facing them, I discovered what silence had been trying to teach me all along: that truth doesn't scream. It waits. It whispers. It invites you to sit still long enough to hear it. When I finally stopped running, I heard the sound of my own heart beating like forgiveness. That is the moment this book truly began.

I am grateful for everyone who helped me find the language to tell it, therapists, friends, mentors, and strangers who offered compassion when I didn't yet know how to accept it. To the readers who see themselves in these pages: your courage in continuing is what gives stories like this meaning. Thank you for walking beside me.

To those navigating their own healing: let silence be your ally. It's not the absence of sound but the space where your subconscious does its deepest work. Listen to the stillness. It knows the way home.

This book is the first in a series of reckonings. What began as an adoption story has become something larger, a study of belonging, of faith, of the patterns that bind and the choices that free. Each book will follow the same thread: that trauma may shape us, but it doesn't define us. That love, when learned through pain, can still become grace. And that forgiveness is not forgetting, it's remembering without fear.

To my children, who are my greatest teachers in love and presence, thank you for reminding me that the story always continues. To the quiet faith that never left me, even when I left it, thank you for the light that stayed.

With humility and hope,

—Will Power

(Author, survivor, witness, listener)

The Will Power Legacy Series

Book 1

We Bought YOU

An Adoption Story That Strikes at Your Soul.

He was raised to believe love had a price.

In the heat and dust of rural Australia, a boy learns early that family can wound as deeply as it protects. Told he was "bought," not born, Will Power grows up under the shadow of a mother whose love is measured in control and a father too weary to intervene. Between chores, silence, and the hum of the fence line that marks the edge of everything, he discovers small sanctuaries in words, faith, and the promise of something more.

We Bought YOU is a haunting memoir of adoption, identity, and survival. It explores the quiet cruelty of narcissistic abuse and the miracle of finding hope where there should be none. At its heart lies one simple truth: we are not what was done to us. We are what we choose to become.

Book 2

Nature vs Nurture

The Reunion That Redefined Everything.

(in development)

After a lifetime defined by silence and survival, one meeting changes everything.

When Will finally reunites with his biological mother, the story of who he is - and who he was told to be - begins to unravel. The woman he meets is nothing like the one who raised him; gentle where the other was cruel, open where the other was guarded. Their connection becomes a living experiment in what shapes us most: the blood that birthed us or the hands that held us.

Nature vs Nurture is a profound exploration of identity, inheritance, and the quiet power of unconditional love. It invites readers to confront the stories they've inherited and to ask: what if belonging isn't something we find, but something we finally allow ourselves to feel?

Book 3

Breaking the Mirror

Understanding Narcissism and the Family

(in the planning stages)

When survival becomes habit, it's easy to mistake endurance for healing.

In Breaking the Mirror, Will Power turns inward to confront the patterns that shaped not only his childhood but his adulthood - the echo of narcissism that reappears in relationships, self-worth, and the search for control. Drawing on lived experience and years of psychological insight, he dissects how generational trauma is passed down like an inheritance and how it can finally be broken.

This is not a story of blame; it's a study of reflection. Each chapter holds a mirror to the subtle manipulations of love and the ways we internalise them. By understanding the narcissist, we learn to stop becoming them - and to reclaim the authentic self-buried beneath the performance.

Book 4

Living a Life Worth Living

The Science of Silence and the Art of Healing.

(in development)

Healing begins where words end.

In the fourth instalment, Will Power explores the intersection of psychology, spirituality, and the transformative power of silence. After years spent surviving and seeking, he discovers that true peace doesn't arrive with noise or victory - it arrives quietly, in presence. Through personal reflection and practical insight, he reveals how stillness activates the subconscious mind, allowing the soul to process what the mind cannot.

Living a Life Worth Living is part memoir, part guidebook - a testament to the resilience of the human spirit and a roadmap for anyone ready to move beyond survival into peace. It is a study of awareness, acceptance, and the miracle of staying.

Book 5

The Company We Keep

Healing Through Connection and the People Who Shape Us.

(in early development)

We are all reflections of the company we keep - the friends who hold us up, the partners who test our limits, and the quiet strangers who change everything with a single moment of kindness.

After years of surviving silence, Will Power steps into the world of relationships with new eyes - not searching for perfection, but for truth. The Company We Keep examines how our connections both mirror and mend our inner world, revealing the ways trauma, trust, and love coexist in the human experience.

From the relationships that wounded him to the friendships that saved him, Will explores the subtle alchemy of human connection - how empathy becomes medicine, and how every person we meet teaches us something about the parts of ourselves still waiting to heal.

Poetic, grounded, and profoundly honest, The Company We Keep invites readers to look at their own circles - to see not just who they've chosen, but who they've become because of them.

www.ingramcontent.com/pod-product-compliance
Lightning Source LLC
Chambersburg PA
CBHW031301090426
42742CB00007B/549